And for All the Sins I Cannot Recall

Autobiographical Vignettes

By Charles Milhaupt

Edited by Merimée Milhaupt Moffitt

Title: And for All the Sins I Cannot Recall

Subtitle: Autobiographical Vignettes

ISBN: 978-057-822-532-6

Cover design by Robert Stokowy

Back cover photo by Merimée Moffitt.

The painting of Charlie's AIDS-ravished face by our sister, Gretchen Milhaupt.

Memoir: Sixties, Gay Liberation, Coming of Age, AIDS, autobiographical stories.

Some mention is made of family and friends still living. Care has been taken to present Charlie's point of view in the Preface and Epilogue; however, that may not be the interpretation others experienced or remember. Though Charlie loved his convertibles, he himself was not convertible. The "facts" in his stories may be contrary to ordinary truth. He suffered dementia, and he was in and out of hospitals continually at the end. His stories were painted with broad strokes and may be best considered to contain a grain or two of truth.

Any profits from book sales, after taxes, will be distributed to
GMHC (Gay Men's Health Crisis) and/or amfAR

Merimée Moffitt, Publishing

Albuquerque, New Mexico

for Charlie

This is a memoir. This is a story about my brother, by my brother: his life in the second half of the 20th century. And he was a 20th Century Fox if there ever was one. This is the story of a handsome, witty man, seeking his place in the world, when he is dying. He had the funniest and most amazing luck. You might call it luck. His fabrications are loosely woven.

Charlie walked in on the ground floor and came out in a penthouse both literally and figuratively, in several endeavors. He didn't do much college, and he evaded Viet Nam; he became a CEO at least twice. He went from messenger boy to producer in Hollywood. He was beloved friend and escort to both Goldie Hawn and Isabella Rossellini. Isabella used to introduce Charlie as her husband. Charlie hung out with Mikhail Baryshnikov and was often mistaken for David Bowie. These famous people were part of his life, and he of theirs. He sought some sense of it all.

This memoir is a love letter to the world, and Charlie lets us know what it was like being him, omitting mostly, any boring parts. He gives us madness and giddy passions. The stories are nuggets, perhaps Hansel's bread crumbs, but Charlie's life was not spared. He didn't make it to finishing his story or having it catch up with him. To some small extent, I fill the reader in on "the rest of the story," in the preface and afterword.

At Charlie's memorial, I managed to claim the manuscript even though Charlie might have decided to just let it go. And then I tucked it away to ripen in the bottom of my big desk drawer. I waited twenty years to let it out of its raggedy manila envelope. What I found surprised me. Faithful to the outcomes of Charlie's other careers, he had beginner's luck at writing vignettes, but they are a mix of wishful thinking and fantasy.

The stories in Charlie's memoir are copied down almost verbatim. Some names are changed to protect the innocent from his indiscretions and inaccuracies.. Nonetheless, the memoir provides a real depiction of life for a young gay man before Gay Liberation in the early seventies, and before HIV/AIDS, ongoing. Charlie shares some experiences about how life was for him. He died March 21, 1998, at age 48, from AIDS, at home surrounded by his close friends and our sister, Gretchen.

ROLL WITH THE CAR

It was 1967, the "Summer of Love," and I was in San Francisco with my best friends, Wayne Fuday and Jay Wilson. We were the core members of a Jefferson Airplane clone called The Hammond Typewriter (a name to which I always objected as being singularly unsexy). We had driven to San Francisco in my parents' brand new Buick Riviera, which had been loaned to me for a week along with a gasoline credit card and enough money to buy tickets for all of us to go to the Monterey Pop Festival, an event of enormous promise that predated Woodstock by several years. I can't really believe it was my parents' idea to provide this opportunity as my graduation gift from high school, but no matter how it came about, we jumped on the chance to take this young Oregonian hippie trip of a lifetime.

It happens that Wayne and Jay and I had been approached by our Neanderthal vice principal weeks before to be told that we were not welcome at our own commencement ceremony because the length of our hair would somehow ruin the entire event for everyone. Needless to say there was a bit more to it than that. Only weeks before I had received the unprecedented "honor" of being named both best looking boy and best looking girl, a school-wide slam at the fact that I dropped out of the popular set in which I had been something of a superstar and had in the second half of my senior year taken on the life and style of a hippie. For this I suffered an incredible amount of abuse from the straight-arrow young Republicans I had left in my pop cultural dust. And again, just prior to graduation, I had caused something more than a stir when I showed up stag at the Senior Prom dressed in a top coat fashioned out of an antique American flag. I don't recall having a dance or a drink or even a snippet of conversation before I was escorted out of the school by one of the more frightening faculty chaperones with orders to report to the vice principal's office first thing Monday morning. Frankly I'd gone to the prom hoping to make a political statement, but little

2

did I know it would turn out to be what is now only too familiarly known to all of us as a mere sound bite.

I'm not sure if my buddies were guilty of any non-hirsute infractions, but I know I was read the riot act that Monday morning. I was told my diploma would be mailed to me and that the entire school (that was 3,000 people minus Wayne and Jay) did not want me present at my own graduation. I reassured my cretinous vice principal that this was super groovy with me because the Monterey Pop Festival was taking place simultaneously and Wayne, Jay, and I had never intended to wear those ridiculous robes and suffer through endless cliché-ridden speeches when we could be watching Jimi Hendrix light his guitar on fire and play the national anthem with his teeth. In other words I managed to confirm the vice principal's worst fears and leave him and Sheldon High School with the feeling that all was right with the world as long as I wasn't around.

So the three merry pranksters piled into the fancy new over-powered Buick, which to this day I can remember had an exterior paint color called "fawn mist," not a color Ford was offering that year. We tore down through the Redwood Highway, driving all night on some illicit stimulant and got to San Francisco (my place of birth) just in time to cross the incomparably beautiful Golden Gate Bridge at sunrise. We were beside ourselves with excitement and self- congratulations on sharing the coolest graduation gift three young rebels could ever hope for. We spent the day in the city walking around the infamous Haight Ashbury district, amazed at all the psycheDelic splendor. Wayne's older brother Bob lived in the Haight and had agreed to take us in for the night. He turned out to be a bona fide hippie god, beautiful, cool, stylish, and surrounded by a harem of the most stunning chicks any of us had seen outside a Bond film. He took us to The Filmore that night, the Mecca of "the San Francisco Sound" where we saw The Jefferson Airplane after having smoked a good deal of Bob's hashish. It was a kind of heaven on earth that I had only read about in Hesse books, a dream I never believed I would actually live.

Somehow our group got split up and I left with Bob and one of his girlfriends, Naomi, a sort of dark-haired Twiggy. We went back to the apartment, smoked some more hash, and then Bob brought out a book called the *I Ching*. This was the occasion for my first full-fledged stoned paranoia attack. The main problem was that I had innocently thrust myself into the vortex of free love without dealing with my own particular sexuality. Nobody, including me, understood that I was gay, but I understood that I felt utterly threatened by any situation that appeared to be leading toward sexual contact of any sort. Well, in my altered

4

state I understood the title of the book that had been so ceremoniously placed in front of us as "Itching" and was fully convinced that we were about to follow some detailed instructions from this mysterious manual on how to create a satiating orgy. Fortunately I didn't bolt from the room, burning important bridges or embarrassing myself to no end. By patiently staying on the scene I shared an extraordinary experience with Bob and Naomi, although I must admit I can only remember the fortune-telling book leaving me with the somewhat obscure information that "The Prince would survive and all the villagers will rejoice." Well at least it was good news. And best of all, I got to retire to my solitary sleeping bag with my unchallenged sexuality intact.

The next day was the opening of the Monterey Pop Festival so we raced off with my three hundred dollars in hand to buy primo tickets to the biggest event midst arguably the most important cultural revolution of the twentieth century, or least a very cool thing to be doing right out of high school in Eugene, Oregon. I'm not sure which of the three of us found the drug dealer in Monterey that day, but it was something like finding a needle in two strands of hay. After a quick check of our available funds and a conference on the relative merits of buying dope or the tickets we had been dreaming about for weeks, we settled on

5

the dope. So now we're in the very place where history is about to be made with a bag full of potent marijuana and only enough money left over to buy tickets to an alternative event billed as "Not the Monterey Pop Festival." So we dragged our sleeping bags out to a field with a little stage just outside the walls of the stadium in which the real event was taking place. We, of course, were ripped out of our minds the whole night, having pretty successfully convinced ourselves that our revised plan was just fine. I do remember, however, one poignant moment when I could hear Janis Joplin way off in the distance wailing "Ball and Chain" while in our foreground at four o'clock in the morning Tiny Tim was doing his second or third encore of "Tiptoe Through the Tulips." Even at the time we knew we had really blown it. We buried our heads in our sleeping bags and got some much-needed rest.

Back in San Francisco we had a few days to hang out before my parents expected us back, so we moved in on Bob and his fabulous crash pad and spent our days at his boutique on Union Square, which was the closest thing to Carnaby Street that San Francisco had to offer. We were laden with hip new outfits and spent our nights sporting our new looks at the Filmore seeing more of the great local groups. The night before we were meant to leave for Eugene, I wandered off on my own to the ultimate hangout, the Haight Ashbury Café, an all-night coffee house that had already been anointed by *Time* magazine as the apex of hippiedom. I was there "hanging out and rapping" for hours while some lovely young waif painted psychedelic designs on my arms, and legs, and feet; I was only blocks from Bob's pad and had for some reason gone off barefoot. I guess I was quite a sight making my way home up Haight Street at four in the morning when a cop car cut me off at the pass; two aggressive policemen jumped out and hurled me against their vehicle and demanded to see identification. Not surprisingly my only ID was the highly original and unique design that now pretty much covered every available square inch of my body. This was neither satisfactory nor even slightly amusing to the officers in question. The stated charge was an unidentified minor (read runaway) out after curfew (I'd never heard the word) possibly on some mind-altering substance (very probably). By the time we reached the station it was clear I was in the middle of a war zone and I was the enemy. So I conjured up every bit of arrogance in me and even in those days of peace and love I was never short of attitude. When the Nazi desk sergeant asked my age I looked him straight in the face and blurted out "two thousand fucking years old, man" a reference to Bob Dylan's recent reference to Jesus. This did nothing to make things easier on me, but it was so worth the moment that the abuse of being pushed and shoved into a cell with a young black boy of thirteen or fourteen who had just been apprehended for robbing a gas station with a gun just felt like more cool civil disobedience.

It was much less cool the next morning when I was awakened with the very sobering news that my mother had flown down from Eugene to retrieve her car and her son (I've always suspected that was in the order of importance—after all she had no reason to be furious with the Buick). I honestly don't remember a moment of conversation during the seemingly endless drive back to Oregon. It would have been impossible to dream up more of a contrast with the trip down. I don't even know how Wayne and Jay got home and was afraid to ask my fuming, hurt, and wildly disappointed mother. Her hands gripped so tightly to the wheel I was convinced she might have a seizure and then, on top of everything, I'd have killed us both. Suffice it to say, this Oregon hippie boy's trip of a lifetime had resulted in the painful but strangely reassuring revelation that no matter what route my life was going to take it was surely no longer going to be under my mother's thumb. She made it exceedingly clear that I was a total disappointment to her and that it was high time I move out on my own and go to college, with which they would be willing to help, or find a job and start finding my own way in life. It was her sincere hope that this episode was just an adolescent prank that was not going to prove to be indicative of a chosen lifestyle and that the shame and self-recrimination I must be suffering (actually I was mostly just a little wasted and missing my friends) would teach me a lesson.

As we wound our way through the majestic Redwood Forest, the more the light flickered through the tall trees into my half-closed lids, the more her voice became a hypnotic drone (albeit in no way meant to be soothing). I started to recall all the trips we had taken on the same route with my two older sisters in the back seat with me, our parents in front usually locked in silent scorn brought on by some trivial disagreement or another. Our salvation was to play a game we called "roll with the car." My sisters, both considerably larger than me, would place me in the center and for miles of winding highway we would allow our bodies to move in whatever way the natural force of the turns took them. I always suspected that the girls did their damnedest to add to the effect so as to be sure and crush me at every possible opportunity. I didn't care because it was such joyous, raucous fun, and it took all of our minds off the cold war taking place in the front seat. So as Mom continued her monotonous lecture about how I was following my older sister right down the path to ruin, I just started to zone her out, and I let go of the door, lifted my left hand from the plush armrest, and started secretly rolling with the car. It was my private little escape from the reality of her hateful diatribe and my little island of joy that carried me back to Eugene, where I was triumphantly reunited with my group, and we all vowed there and then that this was just the beginning (rocky a start as it was) of our magical mystery tour.

SWAN SONG

(1967)

At the height of The Hammond Typewriter's short-lived show business career we were invited to compete in a Battle of the Bands in Seattle, the Pacific Northwest's answer to San Francisco (that is if S.F. were a question, of course). This opportunity was a great honor, as we had up to this point only played relatively small local gigs, mostly for tips and free goods at the University of Oregon Student Union in Eugene. One of these shows was attended by my older sister Merimee, whom I idolized because she was, in my opinion, the consummate hippie. She lived with a legendary musician named Steve Mork who was bigger than life and a close personal friend of The Grateful Dead. I had once

11

conjured up the courage to hitchhike to Portland to see Merimee after a Dead concert when she and Steve hosted a party for them and served marshmallow pies á la "Sgt. Pepper's Lonely Hearts Club Band." I was too nervous to go into the house for hours until everyone was so stoned I might as well have been Charlie Manson for all the impact my pathetic dumbstruck presence made. At least I got to see Pig Pen, Bob Weir and Jerry Garcia up close even if they were in what I would politely call repose and nearly camouflaged with lithe young female bodies in various states of undress.

Anyway, Merimee came backstage after our set in the Student Union. I think I had a couple of solos, "Mr. Tambourine Man" and "Need Somebody to Love," and otherwise sang backup, played my tambourine, and did my best to look sexy and moody like my idol Jim Morrison. She no sooner entered our dressing area than she took me aside to break the bad news to me that I had no soul. Yes, I could carry a tune, and I looked pretty cute, but I was clearly not an artist, and she was sure she was saving me future grief by being completely up front with me, brutal as it seemed. I was devastated and made a hasty retreat. Now this was a real teenage dilemma. I was counting on becoming a rock star and the only real authority on the subject had just declared my aspirations DOA. Mind you, not too deep inside me I knew she was right. I had never really believed in our band and I particularly suffered near crippling self-doubt about my own talent. I guess I figured a thousand screaming fans couldn't be wrong, when in fact they often were, and one wise, experienced, loving sister could be a much more reliable critic, which she was. The big crisis was staring me in the face every day of the following week. How was I going to perform in what was surely to be the most important engagement The Hammond Typewriter had ever booked. I knew I couldn't cop out on my best, and I might add only, friends. I knew I had to put Merimee's pronouncement and my own insecurity out of my mind and just get through the big night. None of us imagined for a moment that we could win, but there was an expected audience of about 5,000 people and we were likely to get very important exposure by simply appearing. Fantasies of record deals and national tours were swimming around my bandmates' heads. So off we went to Seattle in our psychedelic van, checked into a sleazy motel, ate disgusting food and nervously prepared for that night's competition.

At the auditorium we arrived in time to see some of our competitors perform. This, of course, just served to make me even more of a nervous wreck. Out of nowhere, a very hip black guy, who told me he was the bass player in the band up before us, asked if I'd like to go outside and smoke some righteous shit. Now marijuana had a tendency to make me extremely paranoid, but I was already so out of my mind with nerves that I accepted his offer. I was flattered to be asked by such a cool dude. Well it was righteous shit all right, and I barely made it to the stage in time for my first solo, "Mister Tambourine Man." When Wayne, the lead guitarist, realized I was alive and well and on stage, he started the familiar intro, during which time I stood nearly comatose in front of the mike wishing, as the songwriter did, that I could be taken "to a place upon a magic sailing ship." Anywhere but there and then would do. So Wayne just kept playing the monotonous introduction while I looked at him pleadingly to stop and go to another number not requiring my presence. I was a zombie and I hadn't a clue what to do about it in front of 5,000 perplexed rock and roll fans. Finally desperation and a little influence from The Who took over, and I walked over and unplugged Wayne's guitar from his amplifier. Now he was powerless to force me to sing. Unfortunately Jay took up on the bass, as did the rhythm guitars, to try to cover for what they all perceived to be a public professional breakdown. Well, I just unplugged them as well, leaving only our drummer, who launched into a pathetic Ginger Baker-like drum solo that had nobody fooled. Still the audience seemed entranced somehow by the spontaneous madness of it all and had yet to start rioting or even booing. I knew I had only one move left and that was to grab the drumsticks out of the drummer's hands and toss them deeply into the audience. This resulted in an enormous, wild ovation from the crowd, through which I exited having jumped off the front of the stage, never looking back at what must have been a rather stunned group of musicians. I made my way through the audience, took a bus back to Eugene, and went to our rehearsal garage a few days later to apologize and resign from the band. Both gestures were accepted without question, and then I was told that we had won the Battle of the Bands without so much as playing an entire song. Who knows, maybe that was the birth of Performance Art.

WITH A LITTLE HELP FROM MY FRIENDS

On the Fourth of July of 1967 the group of friends that had comprised the now erstwhile Hammond Typewriter had a special event planned. Wayne had been to San Francisco to visit his brother and had returned with a bag full of purple Owsley acid. For the uninitiated, Owsley was the Wizard of LSD and was known for producing in his floating home laboratories a facsimile of what the Swiss pharmaceutical companies had been working on for years. Of course Owsley was selling the drug to recreational users and not dispensing it in a clinical atmosphere in hopes that it might, among other things, cure mental disorders. There was a much repeated but difficult to confirm

17

rumor that Cary Grant had been treated with LSD to cure his homosexuality when he married Dyan Cannon. Frankly, I always figured he needed to take drugs just to live with her, much less fuck her. In any case Owsley was not trying to cure anyone; he was simply making and selling the purist, most potent form of LSD that was on the market in the late 1960s. Purple Owsley was the inspiration for Jimi Hendrix's hit "Purple Haze," the best of the best.

So back to July 4th in Eugene, Oregon, where seven guys who had never tripped before gathered in Wayne's grandmother's quaint Victorian house, left for him to look after over the three-day weekend. We all had read the extensive report on acid tripping that was the *Time Magazine* cover story the week before and felt we all knew all about "set and setting" (taking your trip in a safe place with the right people), appointing someone to be the trip master (the sixties version of the designated driver) and most important, if one of us were to have a bad trip to close the circle around him and talk him through it with love and understanding.

Well, not surprisingly, *Time* hadn't prepared us for this particular day. At about six o'clock that night we each took a half tab and wandered around in excited, nervous anticipation of what was to come. I remember finding a pad of paper and a slew of colored felt tip pens to try to record some of the early oncoming color perception changes. This must have lasted all of a few minutes before I found myself lying face down on the lawn outside, calling for the others to come out and feel the earth move. As some of them joined me it was immediately clear that I was reacting differently to the drug than any of the rest of them. I suspect it was clearer to them than to me because I was busy taking off all my clothes (not something I was ever comfortable doing even in a locker room) explaining that I needed to free myself of any extraneous material goods. I then went into the house, and much to everyone's horror, decided to free Grandma Fuday's knick-knack shelves of all their extraneous material goods as well. It was all very peacefully and joyously expressed, but I was the only one experiencing peace and joy. To the rest of the group, all of whom were high to various degrees, I was being a gigantic bummer, surely having a bad trip and was definitely more than they could deal with. Not to mention that the floor was littered with broken pottery that was going to be difficult to explain.

Apparently at this point (probably around midnight) someone called Gretchen, my eldest sister, a known expert on the ins and outs of acid tripping. I only realized she had arrived when a woman I took to be either Sandra Dee or Joey Heatherton approached me under Grandma's apple tree (understandably I had been thrown out of the house by now) and tried to appeal to me in a soft, mollifying tone that for some reason made me furious, and I hauled off and socked her in the face with a closed fist. At the moment of impact I saw and heard Gretchen's image for the briefest flash, but without any understanding of what I had done. She apparently told the boys that I was way out there, not able to be responsible for myself and should just be kept in the yard all night until I had come down enough to go to sleep. She then left, assuming that one of them would make himself my keeper (what a way to enjoy his first acid trip!) and went home with a sore jaw but no hard feelings.

The rest of this momentous night I've only been able to reconstruct from some glimpses of memory and a few clues inadvertently dropped over subsequent years. What happened was I was allowed to wander out of the yard, stark naked and into an area on the outskirts of the University that was much more populated. I hadn't gotten far before a cop car pulled over and handcuffed me and threw me into their patrol car. What I didn't understand at the time was how Jay mysteriously (and I thought somewhat bravely) appeared to explain to the policeman that I had taken a psycheDelic substance and needed help. He had also brought along some clothes for me and answered all the questions about my identity, my parents' telephone number and address and any other personal information they needed to know. As I said, all of this is a kind of reconstruction in my brain because I was an absolutely somewhere else during the whole trip to the police station. I thought the car was a space ship, the radio a ray gun, and the terrazzo floor of the open courtyard of the recently completed County Jail to be made of gleaming precious stones: emeralds, rubies, and diamonds. It was the Emerald City, only lacking the horse of many colors. I was still blissfully happy and nobody could understand it, least of all Jay, who by this time was more than happy to hand me over to the authorities and get back to the rest of his own trip. I do think he performed an heroic act for me and to my dying day I will always bless him for it.

However, left to my own devices in a solitary cell furnished with a cot and a toilet, I started feeling more and more like being back in Kansas. In lieu of any ruby slippers I concocted a few harebrained schemes to transport me. The first plan (very Glenda the Good Witch) was to connect the ends of my two index fingers and slowly and continuously spell out the word L O V E. That didn't seem to do the trick and I was starting to panic, as I was finally coming down and was increasingly aware that every few moments a new, unfriendly face would appear at the

21

grid in the door to stare at their first LSD catch. My next plan struck me as slightly more reality based and that was to flush myself down the toilet and swim through the sewers back to Grandmother's house. The physics of this solution were of course immediately baffling, and I was reduced to just lying down on the cot awaiting my impending execution.

Suddenly a group of cops entered my cell and shuffled me out of the station into an ambulance and off to the psych ward of the University Hospital. There I was strapped into a bed and visited throughout the night by doctors and nurses who would lean deeply into my face and say "Charles, Charles... are you there?' and various other moronic questions to try to make contact with me. At least they were kind, but I was exhausted and sorry to be their first LSD freak-out and therefore the subject of so much well-meaning interest. I suspected that they too had read the *Time Magazine* piece that had described a mishandled bum tripper who had been given the wrong kind of sedative and was since expected to spend the rest of his natural life convinced he was a piece of orange peel. So no sedation was employed in my case, just constant and annoying observation. But nothing matched the vision of my imposing, Hemmingway-esque father suddenly staring down at me from behind so that I was at the added disadvantage of seeing him upside down. In his deep, imperious voice he announced that he and my mother thought it best for me to spend the rest of the night in the hospital (manacled to a bed in a psycho ward) and that he could come back to get me in the morning when I was more myself. (Fine Dad, but forgive me if I don't wave good-bye because, as you can see I don't currently have the use of my hands).

When I woke up the next morning in a regular hospital room, with no memory of anything that had occurred the day or night before, or in fact where the hell I was, I was completely shocked to see our family doctor, Dr. Schull (a man I had always suspected had close relatives who had stood by Hitler in the bunker until the bitter end). Being the loving caregiver that he was, his only interest was in aggressively interrogating me as to what I took and where I got it. His hideously unprofessional and unsympathetic behavior only served to confirm my suspicions that he in fact may still be working for the SS, posing as a family doctor to get all of our secrets (obviously even at seventeen I'd seen too many bad movies). Anyway I was very tired, especially of Dr. Schull, and asked to be left alone because I was obviously just found somewhere after curfew (a trick I pulled out of the San Francisco debacle) and just needed some rest. With enormous self-satisfaction the bad doctor then told me that if in fact I had not taken any psycheDelic drugs, things were much more serious than he had thought, and he would have to have me committed to a mental institution. Exasperated, but intrigued now to hear what he had to say, I queried him for more information. He nearly gleefully told me that I was apprehended on 13th Street (Main Street, USA) stark naked at three in the morning and that when asked who I was I said with complete confidence that I was The Beatles, all of them! I knew then that he had played his trump card, and I reluctantly admitted to having taken a small amount of LSD, but was under no circumstances going to tell him where I got it. My father arrived and did manage to pry out of me that I had been with my band buddies in a borrowed house and that they were probably still there. Much to my horror he insisted to be taken there to confront the group and grill them on the source of the drugs and assure them that they would be spending no further time with his son. His closing statement was rather unnecessary, since I now know (it took years to piece this part of the puzzle together) that it was my buddies who called the police to take me away and that only Jay had the grace to at least make sure I got clothing and identification so that the authorities could do their job properly. As for the rest of them, I know I was a royal pain in the ass and it was not the first time I had freaked them out, but they did the single most uncool thing a hippie

24

could do to a fellow hippie. They got me busted. They willingly handed me over to the pigs.

In the time that it took for me to put together the whole picture, I saw very little of the group. And on any occasion where we might meet it was clearly strained, more, of course, for them than for me. When I did realize what had happened I never saw any of them again and I'm pleased to report I've never experienced an act of betrayal that's even come close to that of Independence Day, 1967.

FOR LOVE OR MONEY

When the summer finally ended, I tried a semester of college at the University of Oregon. My parents had agreed to let me move into a dorm, and I'd managed to arrange to share with a new friend, Dana Brockway. Dana had the distinction of being the only guy we knew who had been rejected by the draft board at the height of the Vietnam War on the basis of being too thin. He was six feet six inches tall and weighed 135 pounds. None of us, including Dana, understood what his iconoclastic dimensions had to do with surviving the insane, barbaric jungle conditions, but it was not a gift horse he was going to look in the mouth. Another of Dana's peculiarities was that he was convinced he

27

would be late for class unless he slept in his clothes, including, ironically, his combat boots. So each night he slept fully dressed on the top of his bed like a corpse lying in state. There was something so creepy about this. I half came to believe that he was Nosferatu, the undead. Of course, he was just a little weird and lazy.

I took a slightly more relaxed approach to my schedule. When I made it to class at all it was usually to withdraw from the course as I had decided that I was no longer interested in anthropology, for example, and wanted to study sculpture instead. I had started indulging in more serious drugs, like methamphetamine injected into my vein, and on the rare occasion when I could find it, heroin. I stopped going to classes altogether and spent my time painting my dorm room silver along with everything in it, including my stereo, my boots and my leather jacket. There was a definite Andy Warhol idolatry thing happening, but that didn't seem to impress the authorities, and I was told to leave the dorm immediately. Poor lethargic Dana was left with the chore of returning the room to its original "landlord green" and probably got paint all over his only outfit to boot. This was definitely a time of loose ends and personal thoughtlessness (the actual hippie credo—forget all that peace and love shit).

It struck everyone, meaning my parents, that I needed to reconsider my commitment to attending college. Maybe a semester off working at a job would give me time to decide what to do with my future. We only disagreed on one point (well one main point anyway) and that was where and what this job might be. My father thought a few months of pulling eight by ten-foot sheets of hot plywood off of an assembly line for eight hours a day (something I did the summer between my junior and senior years of high school) would be a good idea (and punishment). And, of course he knew just the mill owner who would gladly help him out by torturing me for three more months. I, on the other hand, wanted to go with my friend Donny, who had also dropped out of school, to San Francisco and find much groovier jobs and certainly have more fun. What nobody except me knew was that Donny was the first man I had fallen in love with and that I was about to go off and live with him five hundred miles from everything that had kept my homosexuality painfully in check. So as furious and disappointed with me as my parents were, nothing was going to stop me from making this move. I had much more complicated plans than anyone realized.

We found a funky but big apartment over a dental supply store in the then totally unfashionable Mission District and proceeded to do with it what we could afford and accomplish with our bare hands. I remember seven layers of linoleum came off to reveal a fairly decent wood floor. We argued over some of the paint color choices, but in general we managed to pull together a comfortable pad that we were able to share amicably, if not romantically, as had been my far-fetched fantasy. We were both young and inexperienced in the working world, so finding a job was not easy. After weeks I had become the only Caucasian bicycle messenger in the nation's hilliest city, and Donny landed the unenviable job of proof reading the phone book. At least I was getting a lot of exercise, although this was years before I understood that to be a plus. We were both tired and cranky every night and talked often of going back to Eugene. At that point my sister Gretchen showed up to visit and proceeded to have a hot and heavy affair with Donny. I was somewhere beyond beside myself with rage. I hated them both with an intensity I'd never known. I left, went back to Eugene and didn't speak to either of them for at least a year. I knew then that my life was absolutely not working and I needed to get it together.

My parents were so happy to see me back that they took me in with a minimum of recriminations. They wanted very much for me to try school again and agreed to do whatever they could to help. Unable to return to the University after my disastrous scholastic start I enrolled in the local community college, where I actually attended my classes and even enjoyed many of them. I did so well in math, for example, that I was convinced I would go back to the University once they would have me and major in math with the idea of becoming a math professor. My parents barely recognized me, but were willing to take things at face value since I was regularly getting straight A's, living peacefully at home again and apparently not taking any bizarre mind-altering drugs. Little did they know that I had my selfish bitch of an older sister to thank for this reformation.

It was while I was going to Lane Community College and living the straight and narrow life at home that I ran into an old high school girlfriend who was attending the University. Ellen had always been an honor student, very civic-minded and popular and very beautiful in an overly thin, exotic way. She also had never hidden, at least from me, a tragically sad quality. With all of her accomplishments I knew her to feel unworthy and probably very unlovable. I never remember her having a boyfriend in high school, even though she was a cheerleader and always in the court of every school dance. Her escorts would be some good looking jock or another. I also suspected that she harbored a painful crush on me and that she was too shy to ever make it known. In any case I had rarely been available, since I was always going out with one of the most desirable girls in

31

school after another in order to maintain my status as a super stud. This all ended mid senior year when I dropped out of everything but smoking dope with Wayne and Jay. Ellen and I had, however, been in a few school plays together in our sophomore and junior years and had remained friendly. It was my overt move to bohemia that occasioned her to finally approach me for a date. She wanted me to get her high. I shyly obliged and we had a wild Friday night just before graduation, stoned out of our minds and driving around the countryside in my parents' car at some outrageous speed. There was nothing sexual about the evening, at least not for me, but it was a lot of fun and apparently made an impact on Ellen, since she wrote something in my yearbook a few days later about never forgetting our splendor in the grass at 120 miles per hour.

When I next saw Ellen she had all the style of a classic hippie chick, and she wasted no time coming on to me sexually. We had a few dates, some fairly innocent physical contact and decided that we liked each other. Before I knew it, I had moved into her off-campus house and was sleeping with her. She had become my old lady. One problem however, I refused to have sex with her. For months we maintained this sham of a relationship, each for our own desperate reasons. She wanted a desirable boyfriend (which I can hardly say I was) and I wanted to be like the other

32

guys (not gay). The ridiculous turn of the screw (excuse the unintended pun) was that her terribly uptight, middle class parents were so horrified by our living together in sin that they continuously pressured us to marry. They finally just started outright bribing us and when the bribe got high enough I said okay, what the fuck. And poor Ellen was willing to go along with it. Even more pathetic was that she was acting like there was some legitimacy to the whole ordeal and started planning a traditional wedding.

Now the time came to announce the news to my parents, who had always had their own misgivings about the relationship, but theirs were considerably more reality based. Like for example, they both must have known pretty clearly that I was gay and that this had been a false arrangement from the onset. So over our traditional Sunday night dinner, I made the announcement that Ellen and I were to be married. There was a moment of forced joviality followed by a stunned silence from my mother and some well-chosen words of wisdom from my father. He carefully asked us, in a very rhetorical manner, if what had brought us to this decision was a feeling of life-long commitment to each other, a virtually indefinable bond felt for each other and the understanding that we were making probably the most important decision of our lives. I knew my dad so well that I understood immediately that he was not so subtly expressing his complete disapproval, but allowing us to wind our own pathetic teenage way through his fancy rhetoric. Well, as you know the apple doesn't fall very far from the tree, so I just stared him straight in the face and told him no on all counts. We were getting married because Ellen's parents had offered to double her allowance, give us a car and send us to Hawaii for two weeks.

He caught my drift. We dropped the subject. I dropped Ellen. I was accepted back into the University and moved into a house with Donny and his now girlfriend Patricia. Within weeks I discovered Eugene's only gay bar, The Riviera Room. It was only gay after ten o'clock, but that was good enough for me. So almost every night after ten, I was in the right place at the right time for the first time in my life.

ENGLAND'S FIRST GARDEN CITY

After a few more semesters at school and numerous encounters with not terribly interesting partners from the local gay bar, I decided to take the then requisite semester off to back-pack through Europe. Mind you, at this point I'd never been east of Nevada, but somehow the thought of flying halfway across the world by myself at the age of twenty didn't seem to faze me in the least. Surprisingly, my parents didn't object too strenuously and even matched the money I had saved from odd jobs to pay for the trip. I think that brought the grand total of my budget for a planned three-month excursion to five hundred dollars. Boy, those were the days.

Of course, what I really had in mind was one fantastic non-stop sexathon across the continent. With that in mind I wasted no time arriving in London and going directly to Victoria Station, where I instinctively knew I could get picked up. I was after all a tall, blonde, pretty-boy American with the look of an angel, that only a devil like me could pull off. I no sooner walked into the crowded station than a very presentable looking, smartly dressed black man of about thirty cruised me heavily. I wasn't experienced in the protocol of this sort of thing, but I've come to believe that in gay men it's almost genetic. The pause, the discreet turn to look back, lingering at the nearest shop window to admire merchandise of absolutely no interest. If it's not in the genes, where the hell did we all learn how to do this without ever discussing it with anyone?

In any case, I did all the right things to draw him toward me, at which time he really threw me. I had expected an introduction and some forced conversation leading to an assignation. Instead he just stood next to me and half pulled from his pocket what looked to be a bill of English currency, and one I suppose of great enough value to do the trick. I was actually shocked, not to mention tremendously jet-lagged, and I kind of half laughed at his approach and then introduced myself and told him I was really just looking for a place to stay as I had flown all night from Seattle and was exhausted.

I think he was a little embarrassed by the misunderstanding and very graciously offered to put me up for the night in his home that was a short train ride away. On the train we had a polite conversation about my planned European holiday, my life back in America and some small talk about his profession, which I seem to remember being something rather respectable like investment banking. We left the train and took a short walk through a very conventional, suburban London neighborhood and arrived at his house. It was what we in the States would call a townhouse. I was escorted inside and taken up a flight of stairs, where I encountered a young man who couldn't possibly have looked more like me if he had been cloned in a laboratory. He was Swedish, very pleasant and politely followed our host's request to show me to "the room of love." Uh oh! Now bells really started to go off, and I was getting quite freaked out. I followed the boy down the hall with increasing trepidation as Mr. Smith, as I'll call him, excused himself to change into something more comfortable (no kidding).

The aforementioned room turned out to be a vast chamber of plush red velvet walls covered in enormous homoerotic art and, as its centerpiece, a gigantic red velvet covered round waterbed. The room had been lit with what seemed like enough candles to shoot a scene from "Barry Lyndon" (I suddenly remembered M. Smith had made a phone call before we got on the train). I was speechless, which really didn't matter much since my twin apparently spoke little or no English. I was offered something to drink in sign language and accepted the offer gladly, if only to have a chance to regroup and figure out just how to get the hell out of this mess.

Before Sven had returned with my beverage, Mr. Smith swanned in, dressed in a shear robe (pure Fredricks of Hollywood) barely covering his red satin bikini underwear. Within seconds the robe was discarded ever so theatrically and he approached me, I suppose, thinking he presented quite an alluring visage. He told me that he found me so attractive that he didn't even want to share me with Sven, and we would have the whole night to ourselves in the room of love. I almost fainted. I became very agitated and frightened and said that since I now had not slept for at least twenty-four hours, I really needed to just rest and perhaps we could pick up where we left off tomorrow. He was very pissed off. He demanded to know just what I thought he brought me to his home for. I played dumb and slightly pathetic, and he finally acquiesced and angrily sent me off to a tiny bedroom where I fell into a deep sleep. In the morning he was back in his full business suit drag and was more or less normal again. There was no sign of Sven. I suspected he had spent the night in the dreaded room of love and no doubt needed his well-earned beauty sleep. Anyway I told my host that I wanted to go into the city with him for the day to see London, which was after all what I had travelled eleven thousand miles for, but of course would meet him at Victoria Station at the appointed time in order to return to his house for the experience that he had been promised. He was surprisingly okay with this plan. I excused myself briefly and secretly stuffed all my belongings into my backpack, leaving an empty bag very evidently behind so that there would be no suspicion on his part that I was planning my escape. He seemed to fall for my ruse, and we took the train into London, parting ways with strict instruction as to where and when we would meet for our return. I have never been so relieved to see the last of anyone as he disappeared in the masses of Victoria Station at rush hour.

I found a park bench nearby, sat for what seemed like hours, and suddenly realized I had left in a secret compartment of my abandoned bag my Grandfather's gold signet ring, given to me recently by my mother. I was not only his namesake, and I'm told his spitting image, but I was born three months after his death. At that point in my young life it was my most valued, sentimental, irreplaceable possession. I was crushed but knew that there was no going back, and being such a recently lapsed Catholic, took this as a form of moral punishment. It was, however, a nearly unforgivable tragedy.

Rather than checking into a youth hostel for some much-needed rest like any sensible kid, I continued to cruise the late afternoon streets of London looking for more adventure. This time I was legitimately gazing into a beautiful store window when a very distinguished older man took me completely by surprise by addressing me in German. I didn't know quite how to respond except to tell him that I was not German. He then asked if I were Swedish, Danish, Canadian, all in such rapid succession that it was not really my fault that it took some time to break the news to him that I was a mere American student on a typical, semester-long, European trip. He asked where I was staying, and I admitted that I was on a very tight budget and had yet to find a place that I could afford. Truly this was not a come-on. It was more or less the truth, just slanted a little to the pathetic and needy in case he were interested in helping me out in some way.

He told me I was in luck because he just happened to have recently bought a house in a place called Letchworth (not wild about the name, I remember thinking) and that I could go there with him now and stay as long as I liked. Believe it or not I was back on a train again with a complete stranger headed miles north of London, this time to what he described with great pride as England's first garden city. After what seemed like hours of strained conversation, we arrived in the post-war nightmare. It was incomparably hideous, especially to someone who had grown up in the naturally lush Pacific Northwest. Garden City was a description of planned communities built after World War II with one identical house after another and each with their pathetic little tight-assed garden. I hadn't exactly expected the Chelsea Flower Show, but this place was uniquely depressing.

As we entered his flat I noticed there wasn't a stick of furniture in sight. He caught my reaction and nervously explained that he had just bought the place and wasn't actually living there yet as he hadn't been able to break the news to his mother, with whom it turns out, he had lived his whole life. Brother, can I pick them, or what? So for the second night in a row I found myself in some really bad movie plot. He made a move on me, turned out to have exceptionally foul breath, and I begged off (the breath being the least of the problem). He accepted my stated need for rest and said he was expected back at his mother's anyway. So he suggested I make myself

41

comfortable on his shag rug, and he would be back in the morning with breakfast and god knows what else.

After he left I was so tired that I did fall asleep on the floor determined to get up early and find my way back to London. However, when I went to leave I discovered that I had been locked in and that there was no apparent way to get out because all the windows were fixed. A real panic set in so I rolled up a sweatshirt and broke one of the windows, cutting myself pretty seriously in the process, but got out and fled to the train station and back into London.

I spent the next month and a half traveling throughout the continent alone, reading Dickens, and writing ecstatic postcards home about what a fantastic time I was having. In fact, I think I have never been so miserable and lonely in my life. To this day I have assiduously avoided anything that verges on an advance from an Englishman. That is not to say that I have not returned to England many times and don't have a number of wonderful friends there. I think this was more about my youthful knack for meeting complete weirdos. Now if anything like this happens, which of course is much less likely as I'm older and wiser and don't possess nearly the sexual currency I did then, I would hope to be nearer home and certainly not in any strange country's first garden city.

42

HAPPY FUCKING BIRTHDAY, CHARLIE

Halfway through the European tour, I was sitting one day on the steps of the American Express office in Madrid and an attractive young American girl plopped down next to me and introduced herself. Having stayed so carefully to myself after England, I was kind of relieved to happen upon a friendly soul, especially a female one. She had bought a car in Europe and was in more or less the same kind of uncharted, solitary territory as mine. Her current plan was to drive to the south of France, across the Riviera, down the coast of Italy to Pisa and then inland to Florence and eventually to end up in Rome. She had calculated

43

that all of this would take about a week with plenty of time to take in the sights. I liked her spunk and sense of organization right away. She must have taken an instant liking to me because she asked if I would like to join her for the whole trip, sharing the cost of gas, food, and lodgings. We both admitted to being a little lonely by now and impulsively agreed to leave together the next morning.

She was something of a spoiled American princess, but I'd encountered plenty of them before and made the necessary adjustments to accommodate her nature and have a good time. We drove straight through to Nice the first day, stopping along the way for cheap, Delicious meals. We shared an inexpensive hotel room and toured the whole area the next day. Everything was so beautiful and we were really enjoying each other's company. Typically, I had not told her of my sexuality, but it didn't seem to be an issue, yet. We continued on to Pisa, where I remember we both broke into uncontrollable giggles when we saw the leaning tower. It was just too exactly what one expected it to be. We made it to Florence before we had to stop for another night in a meager pensione. Once again, we shared a room without any apparent sexual tension. Florence was so spectacular that we decided to stay an extra day to see the sights. I made an incredibly foolish error of trying to leave the Uffizi

Gallery with an art book that I'd not paid for and was apprehended by the authorities. I cried and pissed and moaned my way out of it but was more than ready to depart for Rome in the morning.

In Rome we found a slightly grander hotel on which we decided to splurge. Our room was up four flights of beautiful, winding marble stairs and was quite spacious. It was, however, the first time that we were sharing a double bed. I think we both pretended that this was not a problem, after all we were practically like brother and sister by now. We thought three days in Rome would be ideal and then we would decide whether to continue on together from there or go our separate ways.

The morning after our first night in the same bed I noticed a subtle change in her attitude. She was upset that I had made private plans for the day and wanted me to go to the beach with her. I had not come to Rome to go to the beach, having spent my formative years in Southern California, and I was firm in my decision. This infuriated her even more and she stormed off in her car without even so much as a goodbye. I went about my day, which ended in the train station where I had discovered a great pizza stand. I was enjoying just that when I heard my name being screamed from a great distance. I couldn't imagine who it could be and figured there just might possibly be another Charlie

45

amongst the thousands of people in the station. But suddenly I recognized the voice and knew it was hers. She came hurling at me and started to scream expletives at me and beat me with her fists, behaving like a complete madwoman. I managed to calm her down slightly enough to get her story out of her. It turns out that she had felt rejected by me, both socially and more significantly, sexually. Her idea of revenge was to pick up two Italian men who said they would take her to the most beautiful local beach. Instead they drove her into the woods outside of Rome and raped her. At least they left her with her car so that she could somehow get back to the city and miraculously find me to blame the entire debacle on me. I insisted we go to a clinic and have her examined. It turned out she was not injured and was only suffering understandable trauma. I believe she was given a mild sedative and I took her back to the hotel where I put her to bed, packed our things and prepared to leave Rome for anywhere the next morning.

When I awoke she had already moved her bags down to the car. I quickly grabbed my backpack and raced down the steps to join her. She was relaxed, friendly in a strained way, and talked a little about driving north, maybe to Austria. She even mentioned that I had already bought enough gas coupons to get us there so we might as well continue on together. Just as we were to take off

46

she remembered that she had left a favorite hat in the top of the closet and asked if I could retrieve it for her. I bounded up the stairs and opened the empty closet and knew instantly that I had been dumped. I ran to the window to see my belongings lying on the sidewalk and her car disappearing around the corner. I walked downstairs, in no hurry now, and sat down on the curb and realized it was my twenty-first birthday. Suddenly the skies opened up and I was drenched in the most torrential downpour. All I could think was, "Happy Fucking Birthday, Charlie."

THE ONLY QUEER IN TOWN

I arrived back from Europe on Christmas Eve with gifts that I had collected along the way for each of my family. This was something of a budgetary miracle, as I had really tried my best to stick to the five dollars a day plan. I can remember being so strict with myself at times that when I found just the right thing for someone I would either go virtually without food that day or manage a night with no accommodations. It seems impossible to believe now, but knowing then that I was returning just in time for a family Christmas from what was after all a pretty self-indulgent adventure, I felt doubly obligated to be thoughtful. In any case, I had always enjoyed giving loved ones thoughtful gifts. Even at the age of five, when I obviously had no money to buy

49

things for my sisters and mother, I used to crush rose petals and lilac blossoms and put them in jars from the kitchen with a little oil and water and present them as homemade perfumes. I suspect that in that case it was definitely the thought that counted, as I don't remember any of them switching from their regular scents. I think, however, they were very touched by my efforts.

I am sure the offerings that I came home with fifteen years later were almost in the same category, although I believe I did find a beautiful purple velvet hat for my sister Gretchen that she has since remarked upon as always having been one of her favorites. Thankfully she never pretended to leave it somewhere for me to retrieve in order to abandon me. Funny how hats and abandonment have remained connected in my mind all these years.

Once again, I was in Eugene and had to find something to do with my life. Donny and Patricia Williams who had since married, invited me back to live with them and to help them open an English pub. Patricia had studied in Dublin for a year and fancied herself quite an expert in Celtic cuisine. Donny's main contribution was that he had a relatively wealthy and bohemian father who agreed to underwrite the initial investment. I was asked to help design the menu with a very talented guy named John Hurst, as well as to create the logo for the restaurant. Patricia was set on the name Dublin Pub. We all agreed that had the right tone, and so we set forth with our individual tasks. John and I became great friends in the process of designing the menu, and I appropriated some lovely Art Deco lettering for the logo and even hand painted it onto the awning over the terraced dining area at the entrance. It was an exciting and productive time, and when the establishment was ready to open, I was the head waiter and John the chief chef, something he'd been studying as a serious avocation even as he was about to graduate from the university architecture school. The business really took off and grew quickly into the coolest dining spot in town. This, of course, in Eugene, Oregon, circa 1971 is not much of a claim, but it was a success and something of which we could all be proud. We seemed to work all of the time and had no personal lives for months and months. Needless to say, none of us were attending school, not even John, who was a term away from graduation.

Living and working with the same people can often be difficult, but we seemed to manage pretty well. That is until one night at home when Patricia announced over dinner that Donny wanted to have sex with me. I can only assume that this had been previously discussed with Donny, since he showed no sign of being taken aback. Given my history with Donny and the fact that I had at that point never had sex with a woman watching put me somewhere way beyond taken aback. I can't actually remember what, if any, response I had to this announcement. In any case, after dinner I retired to my room and did my best to get some solitary sleep. The next day they both came to me and explained that they had the strong impression that I was attracted to Donny, and that Patricia, as we already knew, was attracted to me and that Donny was open to the experimental encounter involving the three of us. He also pointed out that he loved me very much and I would be the first man with whom he had made love, assuming that I could deal with this proposition. I was overwhelmed with conflicting feelings. Frankly, I was scared shitless. I think I was most afraid that the experience would be a disaster and that our relationships would be irrevocably altered. And of course we were so involved professionally there was the added risk of finding myself out of a job and on the street again. However, I was so desperate to finally consummate this long held torch for Donny that I decided to go through with it.

That night Patricia prepared an especially elaborate meal, Donny chose exquisite wines (which had become his specialty at the restaurant) and I did my best to remain sane. After dinner Donny came over to me and kissed me on the lips. It was an extraordinary moment and it pretty much got the ball rolling. We went upstairs to their bedroom and spent the night making beautiful love to each other. I was fantastically relieved that I suffered no performance anxiety. Whatever inadequacies I no doubt possessed were probably offset by the sweetness and unexpectedness of this shared experience.

Much to my surprise I was asked to join them the next night and the next and next and the next after that. In fact I think my downstairs bed remained unoccupied for at least a month. Then something really strange occurred. Patricia plotted ways to meet me at home during the day in order to have me to herself and Donny started coming downstairs in the middle of the night to slip into bed with me. It was all becoming too much like a market Italian movie for me and, furthermore, I was getting exhausted. I feel compelled to point out that I've never thought of myself as a particularly talented lover, so to this day I don't really understand how this all came about. The oddest thing is that somehow Dana Brockway's then girlfriend, Sharon, a very beautiful and voluptuous blonde girl with whom I had been friends for years, somehow got wind of the situation and decided to get in on the act. Dana worked nights and she would call and ask me to come over and make love to her. I can't imagine that I had much left to offer, but I did spend many nights sneaking out of the house and down the street to Dana's for a middle of the night tryst with Sharon. This all had to stop and indeed it did. For Christ's sake, I was gay and what the hell was I doing? I think I presented an interesting challenge to my friends' wives, it was also the era for such high jinx and, of course, we were still living in that wonderful world before HIV. Being gay was just exotic to these women, not a curse.

It wasn't long after that when I made fast friends with a woman named Liz who thank god was a lesbian. She was smart as a whip and decided that we both needed to get the hell out of Eugene and move to New York City. I just took it on faith that she knew something I didn't, as neither of us had ever been there. Our decision solved so many problems for me that I probably would have followed her to the moon. Donny and Patricia and Dana and Sharon were just going to have to get along without me, and I was going to go somewhere exciting where I understood it was even pretty cool to be gay. I think the only person in this whole cast of characters who truly felt abandoned was poor John Hurst, who was also gay. He just didn't have the same wanderlust that Liz and I shared and was left behind at The Dublin Pub under Patricia's not inconsiderable thumb getting those dinners out night after night and feeling once again like the only queer in town.

TRICKS OF THE TRADE

Liz left for New York in advance of me because I had to withdraw from my working and living situation with a little finesse, which took a few weeks. I think everyone was surprised by my new decision, but as usual, nobody could talk me out of it. By this time my parents, or at least my mother, had pretty much given up on me and was probably just as happy to have me out of her hair.

I had regular calls from Liz encouraging me to come as soon as possible. She had landed a job as a trainee stockbroker right away and said she had met a lot of nice and interesting Wall

Street types already. I didn't know much about New York, but I remember thinking that Wall Street didn't really seem up my alley. She had some ideas about what I could find to do there, but her optimism was boundless and very infectious and although I had something other than what we called in those days "a straight job" in mind, I left for New York as soon as I could.

I arrived at Kennedy airport late at night and was picked up by Liz and some jazzy male friend of hers who drove us into town to a residence hotel next door to the Dakota. The upper west side of Manhattan was so glamorous and exciting that I really couldn't believe I was there. And to be right next to where "Rosemary's Baby" was shot was almost too much. Liz and I stayed there a week before she found a studio apartment in the West Village, directly across the street from St. Vincent's Hospital. We were on the fifth floor and looked right into innumerable patients' rooms. Ironically, this being the era before AIDS, it didn't seem somehow depressing as it would of course now. Nothing did. We were young and in the "city that never stops" after all. And now I was living in a gay neighborhood on top of it. Wow.

I really don't remember how I went about looking for work those first few weeks, or if I even did. Knowing me I probably just went out every night cruising and slept off whatever adventure I'd found a good deal of the next day. I had come with enough money to carry me through about a month before it would be panic time. Liz, on the other hand, was working her butt off trying to climb the stockbroker ladder with tremendous fortitude. That is until the day about three weeks after we'd moved to the Village that she came home early to announce that she had quit her job, answered an ad in the Village Voice and had become a stripper. This was all explained as a reaction to the sexist and chauvinistic quality inherent to Wall Street. She was so totally (and what struck me as suddenly) fed up that she decided what better reaction than to turn one hundred and eighty degrees and work on Forty Second Street in some disgusting, sleazy strip joint. She'd make more money and she could torture the men rather than the reverse. I was certainly in no position to judge her and in fact immediately got in on the act of creating her "character." She was to start the next night and her boss told her to come up with a stage name and a gimmick. With both of us being "Sgt. Pepper's" fanatics, we thought "Billy Shears" would be a funny in-joke, and she wanted to do an S & M thing. Actually, I give her credit for being truly avant-garde with this decision since this was 1973. It was really about wanting to be as punishing to the male customers as possible, in other words, real sadomasochism, not the costume drama that has taken place in the Village ever since.

57

She was nervous but gutsy as hell, I thought, getting through her first night, but seemed to be quite a hit with her unsavory admirers. I had gone to lend moral support, if that's not a contradiction of terms under the circumstances, and I really didn't recognize my Liz. I've never witnessed such a transformation. We subwayed home, she with a pocket full of cash and me bleary eyed and wondering how I was going to fit in my requisite cruising at this hour. I didn't know you could go out at 4:00AM and find plenty of action, but Liz encouraged me to go ahead, as she was too revved up to sleep and would be bouncing around our tiny space for hours anyway. So off I went to the Mine Shaft, about which I heard from some bar mate days before. This was the ultimate gay establishment for late night decadence. There was even a very detailed sign at the door (black, unmarked in any way and in the middle of the deserted meat packing district of the West Village) that had a long list of entry requirements at the top of the dark stairway that mostly had to do with attire. Of course, having grown up a member of a country club, the code was diametrically opposite to any I'd previously encountered. "No designer jeans, no Lacoste shirts, leather shoes only, etc." Somehow I'd been preternaturally inclined to dress appropriately and was allowed in with no question. Inside, I found a world that I'd never even imagined to exist. Room after room of bizarre sexual fetishism in full swing. Fist fucking, which I'd never even heard of much less witnessed, guys being pissed on in bathtubs by dozens of men, elaborate swings set up for all kinds of kinky uses. I wandered throughout the premises and ended up having a relatively conventional sexual encounter with someone on the rooftop (even the experience of having sex outside with a complete stranger struck me as fantastically exciting). I wound my way back through the seemingly endless bacchanalia and out into the barely pre-dawn and deserted streets. As I was walking home a pay phone rang and just for fun, I answered it. A very seductive male voice asked me how I was doing. As it was six o'clock in the morning by now and this was after all a deserted pay phone, I told him he must have the wrong number and started to hang up. He caught me with the phrase, "No, don't hang up. I'm looking at you and you look really hot. Wanna come up?" I looked around me, my heart racing, and saw a lighted window in one of the big converted warehouse buildings on the corner. All I could make out was a silhouette, but this was definitely too much for me, and I hung up the phone and nearly ran home. It had been quite a night. I found Liz asleep in her end of the studio and so slipped into bed with the feeling that now I had truly arrived.

With Liz's career path taking such an untraditional turn I was inspired to do the same. Actually, I wanted to work for

Warhol in the Factory, but I was a few years too late and probably far more wholesome than I imagined. I had met a guy for a zipless fuck a few weeks before who turned out to be an off-duty hustler. He had given me two numbers to call for possible work. One was for a procurer of male prostitutes and the other for a pair of gay porno filmmakers. Needless to say the latter struck me as more glamorous and arguably less seedy, so I made an appointment for an audition. Because of nerves and my habit at the time I swallowed a handful of uppers as confidence builders before my appointment with the filmmakers. Big mistake.

The two guys I was meeting with turned out to be very conventional, polite professionals. Their workspace, full of filmmaking equipment, was attractive, a light-filled loft somewhere downtown. They invited me in and began the interview seating me on the edge of a huge bed, the only furniture in the loft other than their two chairs. We had a cordial talk about my porno movie background, all of which I made up as I went along, thinking I sounded pretty convincing. As we continued to chat, one of them said he was going to turn the camera on for the remainder of our encounter. We talked a bit more and then he casually asked me to remove my clothes and get an erection. Undressing was no problem. However, the second request didn't seem to be in the cards. I supposed they were used to this so they gave me a porno magazine, suggested I relax, take my time and stretch out on the bed. Nothing was happening and I was getting more and more embarrassed. They reassured me that this was not unusual and went about busying themselves with their editing equipment, leaving me to think that this was a full tilt disaster and that the speed I'd taken was contributing greatly to my difficulties. Finally one of them took pity on me and offered me the use of the bathroom for privacy. I took the magazine in with me but could practically see them rolling their eyes with impatience from behind the closed door.

Considering that producing a hard-on on demand was virtually the only prerequisite for the job I knew I had blown it. I was mortified but just couldn't give up. So in the bathroom I tugged away at myself and something, absolutely unfortunate to say the least, occurred. I somehow managed to reach an orgasm without ever getting hard. Jesus Christ, now I'm in this strange bathroom, in an even stranger situation with my clothes outside on the bed with no way on God's earth that I was going to get it up now. Not only that, but the post-orgasm mindset had left me more inclined to climb out the fourth story window than to ever

61

have to face these guys again. But I was just in my socks and I knew I had to brave my way out of there somehow. I reappeared in the room when one of them turned to me fully able to see my limp dick and inquired politely whether I'd had any luck. As I speedily dressed I decided to be honest and tell them about the incident in the bathroom. They were more than civil but I left with the distinct impression that I wouldn't be calling them and vise versa.

I was getting to the point of nearly dire financial straits. Liz, on the other hand, was accumulating tons of money by our standards of the time. She was also slipping further and further into her nether-world of choice; bringing home strip joint bouncers and other strippers for all night poker games. She was happy. I was miserable and desperate and so I looked up the procurer, hoping that he hadn't heard from anyone about my preposterous audition. He turned out to be an exceptionally creepy guy in his mid-fifties, barely dressed in half open Kimono. He looked me over, asked about my experience (about which I lied as well) and decided that I could be his "fresh, all-American collegiate type" and that he even had a john for me that night if I were ready to start. The deal was that I would be paid fifty bucks by the john and half would come back to my pimp. What the hell, I thought, I might as well give it a try.

I arrived that night as scheduled at a palatial Fifth Avenue apartment with a private elevator that opened into a grand foyer. I had only known of such grandeur from old movies. The john was about a sixty-five-year-old, so gentle and well-mannered that I forgot for a moment what had gotten me there. He escorted me to the bedroom where he explained that all he wanted to do was cut holes out the armpits of my shirt (I recalled that my pimp had warned me against wearing my favorite shirt and now I knew why). All he wanted to do for the rest of the hour was lick my fully exposed armpits while he got himself off. Weird, but the easiest twenty-five dollars I'd ever made. I guess I was a hit because he asked for me several more times over the next week. Now I was cooking. Liz was delighted that I had joined her in New York's underbelly. I think she was afraid we were growing apart and that this would now make us something of a team. A stripper and a hustler. How totally hip.

After three or four more manageable tricks I encountered someone so disgusting that I rode home from Brooklyn on the subway sobbing most of the way. This creep had invented an incentive scale for lack of a better term. For each extra and progressively more revolting act I was willing to perform he would add an extra (and unreported) ten dollars to my fee. Without going into gory details I think I was only able to make about an extra twenty bucks before I had to rush to the bathroom to throw up.

I sensed that I wasn't really in the right line of work and so did my next and final john. He too lived in an upper east side palace and was a very refined gentleman. When I arrived he asked if I liked three-ways. I said I didn't know because I'd never had one (there was certainly no reason to bring up Donny and Patricia). He told me that another hustler was on his way over and a three-way had been his plan. I was noncommittal. He offered me a drink which I declined and then asked if I liked smoking dope. I said it made me kind of paranoid and I really didn't enjoy it much. He then sat me down and asked me what the hell I was doing hustling? I couldn't lie to him for some reason and said that he had a good point. The elevator doors opened just then and in walked a muscle bound beauty much more appropriate to the task. My "host" took me aside, gave me cab fare and strongly recommended that I go back to college and get out of the biz. It definitely didn't suit me, or vice versa. I thanked him for his understanding and advice and made a hasty exit. I knew that was my last trick and was greatly relieved.

After a few more non-traditional and very short-lived jobs: a coat-check boy in Manhattan's only gay bar requiring a coat and tie; a bus boy at the Spring Street Bar; and finally, one night as a roller skating waiter at a restaurant on Eighth Street that proudly announced on its sign outside that "Our Food is Great and Our Waiters Skate," I threw in the bohemian towel and went to an employment agency. The only real work reference I could give them was my stint in the plywood mill in high school and my work at the Excaliber . There just happened to be an opening in the plywood division of Mitsubishi International, and I was sent for the interview that afternoon. I suppose my little bit of experience, my faked college degree, and the fact that my father was a wholesale lumberman in Oregon all contributed to the result of my starting there the next day. I wasn't thrilled, more like relieved. I also told Liz I was moving out, her lifestyle by this time having degenerated to the point where it wasn't even acceptable to me. I found a cheap sublet in the East Village and started my "straight job" on Park Avenue, somewhat disappointed that I was now joining the millions of zombies marching to and from work Monday through Friday. My weekends were still my own, and I certainly didn't slow down on my promiscuity. At one point I met a nice man named Michael who lived in a beautiful brownstone apartment on Beckman Place. My month-long affair with him is the nicest memory I have from my New York stay, and although I never loved him I experienced something other than meaningless self-gratifying sexual encounters that were almost always unsatisfying. I don't

65

really remember but I have the feeling that I ended up leaving Michael precipitously and hurting his feelings. Other people's feelings were of minor interest to me in those days, I'm sorry to admit.

A few weeks into my stint at Mitsubishi, word got out that I was a golfer. My supervisor, who had worked there for twenty years, came to me with barely disguised disgust to tell me that I had been invited to join the international vice-president in the following Saturday's Fortieth Annual Japanese Lumberman's Golf Tournament to be held in Fort Lee, New Jersey. I didn't realize at the time that his attitude stemmed from the fact that in his entire term at the company he had not only never met this man, he had never seen him. The international executives at that level worked in a separate tower, accessible only by private elevators and none of them ever entered the plebian part of the operation. As the very lowest on the totem pole of my department, this invitation was unheard of and unbelievable. Of course I accepted, if only to be polite. I had grown up on a golf course and had been a junior club champion and had even wanted to make a career of professional golf until LSD came along. I was afraid my game was going to be a little rusty but I felt I had no choice but to play along.

66

Saturday arrived and I was picked up by limo (my first) on East Sixth Street (certainly my Vice-President's first trip to the East Village). We made polite but very stiff conversation on our way to Fort Lee. I was a nervous wreck and kept worrying that I was going to slip into an acid flashback at any moment. We finally arrived at the country club and went about the business of finding our foursomes and playing the tournament. Much to my relief I had not been paired with the vice-president. I played with three Japanese gentlemen from competing companies. Of course, the entire experience was comported with the ultimate politeness, traditional in upscale golf and even more so with upscale Japanese golfers. I, however, had to concentrate not only on my game but on not having an out-of-body experience; it was all so weird. Surprisingly, I played very well and ended up coming in third out of a field of around one hundred. (I, by the way, was the sole Occidental participant).

At the trophy ceremony when the third prize winner was about to be announced, I was halfway out of my seat, when much to my surprise, the International Vice President of Mitsubishi's name was announced. I was genuinely confused as he confidently made his way to the podium to accept his prize. Later, I asked one of the public relations guys if a mistake hadn't been made in the scorekeeping. He stared me straight in the eyes and said the only mistake would be for me to further question the results. I rode back in the limo and found some way to congratulate my opponent on his completely bogus third prize. He accepted graciously and dropped me off at home. There was no fourth prize, so I came home pretty empty handed. Well, not exactly. The next day, I was told to attend a meeting in the executive tower boardroom. There, I faced at least a dozen of the International Division executives. The speaker for the group told me that Tokyo was intent on Occidentalizing the New York office and that they had decided that I had enormous potential for their executive training program. There was, of course, no question in their minds that I would accept this prestigious honor, so the meeting concluded without my saying a word, and bows and congratulations seemed to go on forever.

Knowing that if I accepted the offer I was making a serious career choice, as well as leapfrogging over my entire department after three weeks, was overwhelming. I had dinner with Liz that night and we talked about all the ramifications of the situation. I went to bed not really knowing what I was going to do the next day, but I did know that I was not comfortable or happy and these seemed like bad signs to me.

Much to everyone's shock (word had already spread throughout the department about my miraculous offer) I turned them down. I made up some story about wanting to return to the West Coast and get my master's degree (no small trick for someone who'd left college as a fifth year sophomore). The executives were disappointed, my supervisor deeply relieved, as I'm not sure he could have survived the envy, and I was even given a very thoughtful going-away party and a gold-plated golf ball with the company logo on it. It's amazing what lying can get you, but it's nothing compared to what it can get you into.

I said goodbye to Liz and the few friends I'd collected in my nine action-packed months in New York City and flew to Southern California, where my father had taken up residence after twenty-eight years of marriage had finally ended in divorce. He agreed to take me in until I could, once again, figure out just what the hell I was going to do.

TRAPPED IN PLYWOOD

(1969)

My father had moved from Eugene to Whittier, California, both the birthplace of Richard Nixon and, more importantly, the home office of his wholesale lumber company. Being born in Glendale and having spent most of his life in Southern California, it was an easy and natural move for him. Furthermore, he was now working in the same office with his two partners and, since business was no longer thriving in the Pacific Northwest, it was a practical economizing effort as well. What was very difficult for him was to be a single man again after twenty-eight years of marriage and family life, imperfect as it may have been.

71

When I descended upon him to share his home, he had already struck up an affair with the condo manager. Her name was Mona, and she was an attractive and agreeable woman in her mid-forties with a daughter in her late teens. She lived in one of the other units and was clearly madly in love with my dad. He, on the other hand, struck me as making do until the real thing came along. I'm afraid he had pretty high standards, ones that my mother never met, and was sure to be breaking Mona's heart one of these days. All of this was apparent to me immediately, but I played along, and even filled in as a fourth in "family" dinners and outings. Mona liked me from the start, and I suspect her daughter had some kind of designs on me that I chose to ignore.

Once again in need of a job, my father introduced me to one of his colleagues at a company called California Wholesale Plywood. Jesus! I was starting to feel like "The Graduate," only the one word for me was "Plywood." I was hired to work in the office as a general assistant to the three or four employees, including the World's most ancient female receptionist, who had a telephone voice that sounded like she was twenty-one years old and looked like Jane Mansfield. She was a riot, and quite a disappointment to first time visiting customers. As soon as I had made enough money, I bought a motorcycle to get to work to save Dad the trouble of getting me there and back. I was, after all, old enough to take care of myself by now. Sure. I started making weekend trips on my bike into Hollywood and cruising the gay bars. Sometimes I'd be out all night and would make up some story to Dad about a great girl I'd met. Who knows if he was buying it, but I wasn't ready for "the talk" just yet.

I'm not sure how many monotonous months went by before Dad and Mona broke up, and he was a desperate bachelor again. He went through every conceivable route to meet a woman; computer dating, singles bars, mixers. Finally, he ran a personals ad in the *New York Review of Books*. That was my dad, no *Free Press* or *Screw Magazine* type he. As he ran his phone number in the ad, and I was still living with him, I was often the first to hear the highly rehearsed voices of some of the anxious respondents. Many of them would hang up when I would somewhat childishly say, "No, this isn't Arthur, this is his son Charlie." In spite of my minor interference, he managed to meet dozens of women and even invited me once to join him on a blind date with a woman who was meeting him for dinner and a play in downtown L.A. It was so strange to sit at the table with him making nervous small talk, while each of us discreetly obsessed on the maître d' station focusing on any single woman who appeared. Finally his date arrived, and I knew, as she was ushered to the table, that she was not going to be my new mom. Funny, how I could make that snap decision for someone else, but Dad and I laughed later driving home about how simultaneously we had responded to her presence. She was perfectly nice, but draped in homemade macramé that she proudly described to us in detail. Also, she was no raving beauty either, and Dad was almost as much of a snob on that score as I was. We got through the evening, but I bowed out of his hunt from that night on.

Out of nowhere Liz called me in Whittier and asked what I was doing. I told her I was marking time, working in dreaded plywood again, and what was up with her. She had come back to the West Coast and was hitchhiking from Eugene to San Francisco, when she got a ride from a guy who turned out to be a Professor of Pharmacology at U.C. Santa Cruz. She was staying with him in a wonderful little cabin in Walnut Creek, and he was dying to meet me. Why me? Well, Liz explained, she had discovered that she was bi-sexual, and, guess what, so was he. She also told me that he was beautiful, brilliant, and had an over-flowing case of pharmaceuticals with which he was very generous. Good-bye Whittier. Good-bye Dad. Good-bye plywood! I was on the next plane to San Jose, and one of the sweetest things my father ever did was, without apparent judgement, drive me to the airport and, at the last minute, give me a camera with a request to send him pictures from wherever I went to share with him whatever I did. He was really one of a kind, and I was, only then, starting to understand that.

Liz and Tony met me at the airport, and we walked through the terminal shyly checking each other out, while Liz glowed with excitement. We came to a water-cooler and Tony dug a large white tablet out of his pocket, placed it on the end of my tongue, and gently guided my head to the flowing water. Unknowingly, I had just swallowed my first Quaalude. The drive to Walnut Creek was about an hour, and I think we were already having sex on the road, well before arriving at his charming little mountain cabin. Needless to say, none of what took place in the next few days was documented for my father. Mostly, we got stoned and fucked, (Tony and me, and Liz and Tony, but never Liz and me; that wasn't part of the deal). We did all share a bed, and eventually Tony had to go to work, but would assiduously dispense our "medication" before leaving, and we would be hopelessly stoned the whole time he was away. We would try to accomplish the simplest things, like doing laundry, or walking into the nearby little town to eat or shop, but would find ourselves in useless piles of giggles, or completely passed out somewhere. We were happily trapped, and even guarded by a German Shepherd that Tony left behind to keep an eye on us.

I can't remember which of us started getting paranoid first, but it hardly mattered the morning I woke up to find the barrel of a pistol held to my temple, in Tony's hand. He had a demonic look on his face, and wanted to know if I was fucking Liz while he was away at the university. I froze, and then promised him that Liz and I were like brother and sister, and nothing could be more unlikely. Liz got hysterical and Tony backed-off. He dressed for work and gave us our drugs as usual, and said he'd be home early. We went into a wild panic, didn't get stoned, and tried to work out some kind of plan. The dog, it turned out, was also trained to keep us there. Every effort to go outside was met with a threatening growl. We were completely freaked.

When Tony got home we did our best to act casual and natural. We got through the night, but noticed that, in the morning, Tony left for work in his usually professorial attire, accessorized by a face fully made-up with Liz's makeup. He was going off to the University of California at Santa Cruz to teach a class on Pharmacology to a large group of graduate students dressed thusly, and, as Liz and I had surreptitiously not been taking our 'ludes the last couple of days, we were sober enough to know that we were in the grips of a real madman now. He kissed us good-bye, as if nothing were amiss, leaving big red lipstick stains on our faces, and departed. We were out of there, even if we had to kill that dog. It turned out that in our stoned state, we had overestimated his power, and managed to throw our things together and get on the next bus to San Francisco.

We deposited ourselves on Margaret William's doorstep (Donny's fabulously eccentric librarian mother), who took us in and sat fascinated, over strong coffee, hearing our exciting tale. The very next day, the headline in the local San Francisco newspaper read "Walnut Creek...Murder Capitol of the West!" The story was that twenty-eight bodies had been dug up in the woods outside Walnut Creek, in the vicinity of Tony's cabin. Liz and Margaret and I couldn't decide whether to laugh or cry about us possibly having been numbers twenty-nine and thirty. It seemed highly unlikely Tony had anything to do with these murders, but, at this point, anything seemed possible. Margaret invited us to stay with her as long as we liked, and, as she lived in the Castro District (Gay Town, USA), it seemed like the right thing to do. We were certainly in no shape to make another immediate move and so we accepted her kind offer.

The very next afternoon, I wandered into a Castro Street bar called The Midnight Sun. It was pretty much an all-day and all-night place, and very much the pick-up place of the moment. On my first foray inside, I made it half-way down the bar, when a man leaning against the wall grabbed me and kissed me passionately on the lips. He was extraordinarily beautiful, with shoulder-length dark brown hair and the face of an absolute angel. As off-guard as I may have been taken, I didn't resist in the slightest. It was surely the closest I'd ever come to love at first sight, and I had the strong sense that it was mutual. We talked, and drank, and kissed, and held each other for hours, before leaving the bar together to go to his house. I just decided that Liz and Margaret would understand, and didn't give it another thought.

When we arrived at Tommy's, I was mind-boggled by his living arrangement. It was a second story apartment with a first-floor entrance opening from the street onto a flight of stairs that led up to a world, the likes of which I'd never seen. The huge space was full of beautiful antique toys, some in display cabinets, and others just scattered around on the floor. Antique tricycles, old-fashioned beach balls, an environment of unparalleled eccentricity. Tommy reveled in showing me his favorite treasures, and I couldn't have been more enthralled by it all. He suggested we share a bath, (something I'd never done) into which he brought a whole German chocolate cake. It was hilarious, and sexy, to gorge ourselves in the bath, making a mess and having a ball. I can't imagine we were getting very clean in the process. We were undoubtedly stoned, because we forgot to turn the water off and the tub overflowed so badly that it leaked through the downstairs neighbors' apartment. Apparently, Tommy's bathroom was above their living room, and the water filled an elaborate antique chandelier, shorting-out their electricity, and the next thing we knew, there was frantic banging and yelling coming from the bottom of the stairs. We jumped out of the tub and Tommy grabbed the two items of clothing hanging from the back of the bathroom door: a clown suit and a fur coat. He slipped into the suit, and threw the fur coat to me. We went tearing down the stairs, looking like we were on our way to a costume party, and found a furious old queen, (this was not Tommy's first infraction as a neighbor), complaining that, if this ever happens again, he's going to have Tommy evicted. I was a little embarrassed to be introduced dressed as Tallulah Bankhead in "Lifeboat," but we did our best to mollify the guy, and promised it would never happen again. We climbed the stairs in a fit of barely controlled giggles, and fell into each other's arms, rolling around with the toys like lovers in the circus. It all felt so light and joyful, after the bizarre heaviness of Tony in Walnut Creek, that I was out of my mind with happiness.

It was only then that I noticed all the paintings on the walls and scattered around the apartment, leaning here and there in various stages of completion. They were spectacularly beautiful, and all paintings of cows. I asked, and of course, they were Tommy's work. I was so impressed and happy that this beautiful, strange creature was also an exceptionally talented artist. He was my dream man. How quickly a dream can become a nightmare. The only warm spot in the rambling apartment was the kitchen, near the gas stove, which was always left on for heat. Tommy laid a blanket down on the floor, and proceeded to make love to me as I'd never experienced it. I'd never been fucked before, and it was so natural and painless and beautiful that I cried with joy. Tommy was my angel. Suddenly, we heard what sounded like a brick or a stone being thrown through the transom window above the downstairs front door. A deep male voice was yelling drunkenly, "I know you're up there, and you have that little dancer with you. Let me in, you two-timing piece of shit."

Tommy put his hand over my mouth, and led me quickly to a closet, without any explanation. He closed me in, and I didn't hear anything again until the intruder had made his way through the window and to the top of the stairs, where he started abusing Tommy verbally and physically. Tommy didn't seem to be defending himself, from what I could glean from my hiding place. But, suddenly I heard things crashing and realized that all of the display cabinets encased with precious toys, were being knocked over and destroyed.

80

"Who the fuck do you think pays for all this, you little shit? Whose apartment do you think this is, anyway? I suppose that you've told your trick that it's all yours?"

Poor Tommy. My heart was racing, and I wanted to burst out to protect him from this monster, but I was so physically afraid I was paralyzed. Then, my conundrum was solved when the door was suddenly thrown open, and a man in his mid-fifties, dressed in leather from head to toe, grabbed me, throwing me to the floor near the top of the stairs.

"So, you're the little dancer Tommy's been fucking." He was crazed; (I'm neither little, nor a dancer, but that didn't seem worth pointing out at the time). He told me everything was his: the apartment, the toys, the paintings, and most importantly, Tommy. I was to get, and stay, the fuck out.

For the first time in my life, I was so angry I got into a violent fist-fight. I was going to protect Tommy if it killed me. We were perilously close to the top of the open staircase, scuffling with each other, when I realized I was covered in blood. I jumped back and gasped, and he laughed at me and said it was his blood. He had cut himself badly, climbing through the transom window. This sort of stopped things for a brief moment, at which point the police arrived, (the downstairs neighbor, again) and we rushed to dump our dope down the toilet, and then let them in.

They took Tommy's "friend" away, and told us to just keep it down, and disappeared into the strange night.

Tommy was full of self-recriminations and apologies for not having explained his situation with this guy. He was terrified I was going to reject him now. All of this conversation was taking place, of course, amidst the most chaotic rubble imaginable. So many beautiful things destroyed. But not my love for Tommy. If anything, I loved him more because he was so vulnerable, sensitive, and needy, that he would let a creep like that help him so that he could do his art. Thank God, none of that had been damaged.

We talked about what to do, and I impulsively invited him to come to Eugene and live with me. He admitted that, not only had he never left San Francisco (since birth), but, that he was on a government program that provided a minor stipend to the "psychologically dependent," so that, even without this questionable "patron," he could survive, providing himself with the basics. I think he'd been on this program for four or five years, and it required him to reside in the city, and to ask permission for any time spent away. He also had to see a government psychiatrist once a week, to evaluate his condition. Apparently, in the post-sixties San Francisco era, this was a thriving program.

It had never even occurred to him to leave, as he had been born and raised in the city, and part of the mental state that occasioned his need for government support, was probably some kind of agoraphobia that kept him inside the city limits, regardless of official regulations. Amazingly, given my inquisitive nature, I accepted his explanation and just went into gear trying to help him out of the mess he was in. We cleaned up the apartment and got a little sleep. In the morning, we made beautiful love again, and then I took him to meet Liz and Margaret. They both recognized him as special, a sweet soul, and were instantly happy for me. They didn't get the insane back-story until later, but even then, they were encouraging. They could see I was head-over-heels in love and it made them so happy.

He stayed with us that night, and the next day he asked his shrink if he could move to Eugene with me. The good news was that, when he showed him a picture of me, the guy told Tommy that I looked like a kind and gentle person who could be trusted. (He, obviously, knew about my predecessor). The bad news was that, if Tommy left, he would be taken off the program, and more significantly, that he would be leaving the only place he'd ever known for thirty years. This was a big decision, and understandably, the psychiatrist suggested that Tommy give it considerable thought before taking any action.

That night we all had dinner out in the Castro district. Margaret regaled us with wonderful tales. I remember a moment when she said, in a voice loud enough to be heard by a number of surrounding male-dominated tables, that she had attended Carmen Miranda's wedding. It was like one of those stock-market commercials; sudden silence all around us, with all heads turned in avid fascination. She also told us that she had been doing an unofficial study of butt shapes in the Castro District, and had come to the conclusion that men, in general, have much prettier shapes, and black men in particular. Well, she was a sixty-year-old librarian, after all, so we forgave her restatement of the obvious and found it irresistibly cute. We had a wonderful night, and everyone was easy and comfortable with each other. I knew I wanted Tommy to come to Oregon, but I also knew it was a really big deal for him, and that he was going to have to make up his own mind about all that.

Liz and I left the next morning, after my exquisitely painful good-bye to Tommy, and went to stay with Gretchen, who had an extra room on the top floor of her house. The Excaliber immediately took me back as a waiter, and Liz found something to do and moved into her own place within days. I think she was hoping to make room for Tommy. He and I talked daily for a week, and finally he announced he was coming. He put his paintings in storage, withdrew from the government aid program, and was coming to Eugene to be my lover. MY LOVER! Oh, my God. Not until that moment had I really considered that I had not only never had a lover, but I had never been openly gay in my home town. I was so excited about him joining me, especially taking into account all his personal complications and sacrifices. I quickly buried my nerves and existed on blissed-out love and giddy anticipation. I told my sister and my close friends that my first real boyfriend was moving up from San Francisco to live with me. Gretchen was sweet and said we could live in her attic space as long as we needed to, and Patricia said if anything appropriate became available at the restaurant for him, she'd of course, hire him. Things looked awfully good.

I met Tommy at the bus station three days later, and we fell into each other's arms, both of us nearly drowning in joyful tears. Fuck the bus driver's attitude. Fuck everything. We were together, safe and madly in love. We drove to the house, and Gretchen was lovely and gracious, and made him feel immediately welcome. We made love in our little attic nest and got him settled in; he'd come with very little in the way of belongings. We then went to the Dublin to meet the gang. Everyone took to him and was so happy for me. They could see I was glowing, and it was infectious. Of course, Tommy was having his own experience, probably almost psychedelic. Everything was new to him: the locale, the people, our relationship. It must have been overwhelming. On top of it, I'd never even asked him why he was on government psychological aid in the first place, so he was probably facing all these intense changes at an added disadvantage, as well.

The first few days, when I was at work, he stayed home reading, staying pretty much to himself. Gretchen reported to me that she found him very quiet and withdrawn, but clearly a good person. She thought I could trust him, and that was what really mattered to her, for my sake. I, on the other hand, had quickly found myself being followed around by him, like an adorable but helpless puppy dog. He seemed incapable of making decisions, or doing anything for himself. I had always been such an independent sort, that this quality of Tommy's started to drive me up the wall. I was panicked. I think I knew I'd made a terrible mistake, dragging this gentle, damaged soul away from everything he'd ever known, into my world, where, frankly, I turned out to be unprepared to take care of him. After another traumatic day, I sat him down and told him the truth. He was going to have to go back to San Francisco, (I would give him all the money I had made in the previous week at the restaurant,) and that I was truly heartbroken that it had not worked out. We cried, (this time, not joyfully,) and held each other, but I think we each understood why it had to end, even so abruptly. I saw Tommy off at the bus station the next day, and I have never been so sad. So many factors were involved in the failure of the experience that, to this day, I've never really worked it all out. I also have never been without Tommy in my heart somewhere, and every so often, especially when I see a cow or a particularly beautiful antique toy, the whole experience comes flooding back into my mind, and I'm so happy again about the day he swept me into his arms, and his crazy life. We shared a whirlwind romance that remains, forever, a moment of magic in my long life.

HOLLYWOOD SIGN

(1969)

There wasn't much to keep me in Eugene after Tommy left. Liz had decided to go back to New York to finish college, and I was still drifting. Something made me head south to Los Angeles (a decision most Oregonians would equate with choosing to go to hell). I had spent enough time there during my stint with Dad in Whittier that I had a hunch I could get something going in L.A. I felt like I was finally starting to grow up and that maybe it was time to start thinking in career terms rather than just jobs to get me by. Once again, I bid farewell to the D. Pub crowd and left for California. I was not entirely without a plan, as I had contacted a guy I'd met in New York and become friendly with

89

named Luis. He had moved to L.A. a few months earlier to work for a famous film director, a good friend of his, as a publicist. As this director loathed publicity of any sort, I came to kid Luis that he was Hollywood's only "suppress agent." Anyway, Luis essentially had the job because he was an extraordinary fellow, a quality he had made into his life's work. He was born in Puerto Rico, educated at Oxford, and had a law degree which he used to teach but never practice. He was such a unique character that if you asked five hundred people to describe him, each of them thinking he or she was his closest friend, you would get a different picture from each of them. He thrived on intrigue and gossip and insisted on remaining an enigma to everyone.

Enter Charlie. Luis asked if I would like to share the rental apartment he'd taken in the Hollywood Hills under the famous sign. It was charming as hell and had a very nice second bedroom. I arrived and moved right in and everything was just dandy. Luis seemed to be "working" at home a lot and the phone never stopped ringing. I noticed that for the first week or so that when he was apparently asked "Who was that who answered the phone?" he dismissed these banal inquiries with something like "Oh, that's a boy staying in my spare room for a while." I didn't take offense, I just found it notable since I was paying half the rent.

Shortly thereafter, he sat me down for "the Talk." Luis told me that since I was gay and he was straight that he didn't want there to be any misunderstandings or sexual tension in the house. I was speechless, as I had never even considered him in sexual terms. But I let him speak his peace and assured him that none of this would be a problem for me. I told him again how happy I was to be there and that all I needed now was a starting job in the movie business, and I might be finally on my way.

I think it was three nights later that my bedroom door opened at midnight and there was Luis in silhouette, just standing there motionless. He had awakened me, so I sleepily asked if anything was wrong. He sheepishly admitted that he had fallen in love with me and wanted to come into my bed. Well, after how carefully he had outlined the parameters of our relationship, I was puzzled to say the least. But in my own way I had come to love this strange individual over the last few weeks and I invited him to join me. The lovemaking was very shy and tentative and really quite sweet. I think he'd had some previous experience with men but at the time I imagined it was probably boys school stuff. Now he was with someone with whom he was living, and looking back I think it was a very brave move on his part.

Within a few days Luis had introduced me to a friend of his working at a prestigious television film production company. They made the kind of movies for television that always won lots of Emmys. Renee was the assistant to the production coordinator and they needed a new gofer (go for this, go for that). I got the job that day and was immediately sent off on a million different urgent errands in a company car in a city I didn't know with never enough time to accomplish my daily myriad of tasks. Renee was tough and aggressive and took a liking to me because I wasn't a lazy dope and could get the job done. I quickly caught on to her act however. She was intent on becoming a producer and spent most of her time misrepresenting herself as an executive at the company and setting up pitch meetings and trying to option books and scripts. She barely did any of the work she was meant to do so that got split between me and her superior, Judy, a born slave who had been having an affair with our married boss for seven years and still dreamed that he was going to marry her. He was a classic Hollywood pig whom I never liked but of course managed to get along with. Because I had to cover for Renee so much I did an inordinate amount of office work for a Delivery boy and people took notice. It didn't stop anyone from sending me on degrading errands, like the day I was asked by one of the social-climbing, in-house producers to return a cleaned casserole to Henry Fonda's house from what must've been a pretty upscale covered dish dinner the night before. Not knowing how these Beverly Hills mansions function, I walked right up to the front door, rang the doorbell, and stood there feeling kind of a jerk with this dish in my hand only to have Henry Fonda himself open the door. I kind of went stone dead, muttered something unintelligible about the man who'd asked me to return it and raced to the car. I don't think the poor man had encountered such a bundle of nerves in some time. My other absurdly noteworthy assignment was when I was told at three o'clock in the afternoon I had to take a contract to Palm Springs for Truman Capote to sign and be back before six o'clock. Well, it is possible to get to the Springs in an hour and a half (of course I'd never been there before) but to get out of Truman Capote's living room in less than an hour and a half was the real trick. He never got off the couch, was served one drink after another by some attendant, and having made the mistake of trying to be polite I said something about never having been to Palm Springs before and how bright the stars were. Capote looked me up and down, told me I looked damn sexy in my leather jacket, and that I should never for a minute think that those pathetic things backin Hollywood that called themselves stars are anything but cry baby pieces of shit. I declined his third offer for a drink and became really quite insistent that I had to rush the signed documents back at a highly illegal speed or lose my job. He acquiesced and let me go, unmolested and charmed to death.

There's just one more spectacularly goofy errand that's worth mentioning that made urgent sense of my need to move up the production ladder. One of the company producers traditionally sent poinsettia plants to fifty of her colleagues scattered all over Los Angeles. What was especially cute was that they all had to be Delivered on Christmas eve. A good many of the plants, all sitting upright in the back of the station wagon, had to make it intact through Laurel Canyon. Well, pulling this off successfully would have been something like winning the grand prize on Beat the Clock. At every hairpin turn, of which there were many up and down the canyon, any number of pots would fall over and the stems would snap. So ultimately a large number of this totally unappealing and quite successful (a familiar combo in Hollywood) producer's nearest and dearest received dead poinsettias stuck into their pots, which with any luck made it through Christmas dinner. I've always hated Christmas as an adult and especially poinsettias, as they are among other things poisonous, so although I would have preferred to have done a good job for this witch, I kind of enjoyed the anti-Christ(mas) part of the deal. And, most importantly, I never got caught—rule number one in Hollywood.

So Renee quickly moved up and out and I was tagged to take over for her job in the office. I was happy because it got me off the road and Judy was thrilled, since she actually had some real help now. I was really starting to learn about the nuts and bolts of production, even if it was from guys whose brains seemed to be comprised primarily of nuts and bolts. In the meantime Luis and I continued our affair, although I still heard myself described as the boy staying in his spare room, and, of course, never met his fancy friends. I think I was once taken to Peter Fiebelman's house to swim but only after Luis had established that Lillian Hellman was not going to be there.

Then Luis pulled the strangest thing on me. He told me that although he had thoroughly enjoyed our physical relationship, he now felt he needed to experiment with others, branch out. I couldn't actually blame him. It was, after all, the era of wildly promiscuous gay sex and there was a whole buffet of beautiful men out there from which he could choose. Also, Luis had a secret weapon in the war between the same sexes. He was prodigiously endowed. So much so that with my narrow palate and unaccepting asshole we mostly had to settle on mutual masturbation long before it became fashionable. There was one

95

funny night when he begged and begged to fuck me and I finally gave in and smeared what I thought was Vaseline all over his huge dick when in fact it was Vick's Vaporub. He was in complete agony and I couldn't help but laugh and laugh. It definitely got me off the hook.

The truth was that Luis had so little gay experience before me, he didn't know the basics of getting picked up. So like some kind of deranged Pygmalion he asked to be taught how to "cruise." I couldn't take him seriously at first and laughed him off. But he was serious. Don't forget now, I'm about to give lessons on how to get laid to the man who is jilting me. I think there was something so genuinely innocent about his character that allowed me to go ahead, not only without much acrimony but actually getting kind of a kick out of the silliness of it. We had a long living room and I literally walked him through the mechanics of picking up an interesting stranger, right down to every formulaic detail.

We stopped sleeping together that night, and several nights later he came home and announced with great self-satisfaction not unlike Miss Gooch in *Auntie Mame,* that he had cruised! I suppose I was meant to congratulate him and ask for the gory details, but by now, reality had set in and I felt abruptly sexually and emotionally rejected and a bit responsible for turning Luis into some kind of Fagenstein. Over the next few months there seemed to be an endless stream of boys and men drifting in and out of Luis's life. My feelings had really been hurt and there were far too many bodies floating around the apartment for my liking.

Possibly the most unlikely turn of events happened then. I met and fell in love with a young Australian woman. She was terrifically sexy and something of a playgirl surviving on a monthly stipend from her wealthy, indulgent parents in Sydney. The story gets more labyrinthian. Jilanne was married for immigration purposes to a man named Richard, who was the film critic for L.A.'s lesser daily newspaper. He was an outrageous, hilarious queen whose major claim to fame was that he had been a Mouseketeer. Actually, he was still something of a Mouseketeer, only his clubhouse was filled with decadent drug addicts and thrill seekers, whom Richard kept well stocked in the recreational drugs of the moment and held wild gatherings for them every night. He was really a pathetically lonely soul determined to be the life of the party if it killed him. Unfortunately he fell for me in a big way and when Jilanne and I started our affair it almost did him in. I remember driving away from his Laurel Canyon house in the middle of the night to take Jilanne home (after consuming enormous amounts of his drugs, no doubt) with him standing in the middle of the street screaming how much he hated us. We did feel for him, but we had discovered this unlikely love and nothing was going to stop us.

Funnily enough, Luis seemed more appalled than Richard by our affair. I must admit we behaved as if we'd invented heterosexuality and could not be deterred from going at it at any time in nearly any place. All of my friends were confused to say the least. Actually, the sexual part ran its course in a matter of weeks, but the friendship went on for years. In fact, it was our decision to find a house to share that finally got me out of Luis's apartment and life.

So on the 4th of July, 1976, Jilanne and I moved into a wonderful little adobe in Echo Park and lived there together for better or worse for the next five years. I wasn't living under the Hollywood sign anymore, but I definitely had Hollywood in my blood and something big seemed bound to happen.

PORTS IN THE STORM

Something very big did happen just as I was really making my presence known to the big boys in the company. The parent company, with no prior warning, withdrew all of its financing and we were all out of a job overnight. Of course, the suits all had fat contracts to be settled but someone like me was out on the street with what remained of the last week's payroll check.

I was in pretty dire straits and rather than confidently take my reasonably impressive, if brief, resume to alternative companies I sort of panicked and over an afternoon drink at a local industry dive called Ports I casually asked the owner if he needed any waiters. I was falling back on old skills and knew that

99

if I got the job it would be temporary until something came up in the business again.

The owner, Jacques Livingston, was quite a character. He was a three-hundred-pound, alcoholic diabetic who was the black sheep of THE Livingston family. He had grown up all over the world, spent his childhood on his grandmother's grand ranch in Brazil, for example, was a connoisseur of fine wines and haute cuisine; and owned this truly sleazy restaurant that was an established hangout for Hollywood's second and third echelon. I found out later that he was the black sheep of the family primarily because he had willfully married a Jewish woman from Boston named Michaela. None of the Livingstons could accept this choice, not that there weren't plenty of other things about Jacques that one would have a hard time accepting. He, on the other hand, accepted me as a waiter starting that night and asked me to come early, as he would want me to shop for the food at the nearby market. I didn't really take time to think about it and showed up in the requested attire (very traditional black pants, white shirt and black bow tie) and went rushing out to Ralph's Market on Sunset with four hundred dollars to do the shopping for that night's dinner. It was kind of like "Supermarket Sweep"; Dolores Diamondwould definitely not have approved. Jacques' theory, if he really had one, was that the food was fresher, and we only bought what we were going to use. A little more expensive than wholesale but less waste.

After the shopping was done I would set up the restaurant with another waiter and a busboy. The place was packed every night with has-beens and wannabes and an occasional curious tourist. It was, after all, the last bastion of bohemianism in Hollywood. There was one semi-established film director named Henry Jaglom who would eat there regularly with his girlfriend. Only the most junior waiter on shift was willing to wait on them because they had an elaborately choreographed routine to insult and mistreat the waiter, hoping, I suppose, to reduce him to tears, for their entertainment pleasure. Given how forgettable his movies are, I guess he had to find some other creative outlet, but this was a really disgusting display of highly thought out cruelty. It's just the sort of thing that spurs one on to become more powerful in the movie industry than he was (which eventually I managed to do).

Michaela was a major character on her own. She was addicted to Ritalin, a mood elevator that was a super stimulant. In her rattled way of speaking she sort of cocked her head as she reached into her jeweled pill box and referred to it as "the beveled edge darling, the beveled edge." Of course, I never turned down an offered dose, which would make my shift

101

considerably more manageable and more fun. It didn't stop there. I was also using a lot of my tip money to buy cocaine and Quaaludes and getting into the habit of working in a highly altered state. Since Jacques was so blasted every night from his fifth of scotch, he was in no state to judge my sobriety. Actually it was all a bit of a game for me, since the job itself had become so monotonous after a few months, with Jacques being contradictorily demanding about the elegance of our service, I was able to amuse myself by trying to live up to his absurdly high standards completely loaded. For example, we were not allowed to write down any of the order, so when waiting on a table of eight involving drinks and first and second courses, it became a personal challenge, like the Sunday *New York Times* crossword puzzle, to remember everything correctly. Needless to say this all led to a bad end. Two incidents of note are the night I fell asleep across a table of four highly uncomfortable customers for god knows how long, and the other being that when some impatient diners felt that they had been kept waiting far too long for their check (which I'm sure they had) I yelled for the entire place to hear that "This isn't Bob's fucking Big Boy and you'll get your check when I feel like it." I think we all knew my time had come at Ports, but it had served me well. I had paid the rent and the bills for nine months and, except for my increasingly out of control drug habit, I had survived unscathed, even Henry Jaglom.

What to do next, the never-ending theme of my life, was now the issue. And, as usually happened, something promising just came out of the blue. I was hired to assist the production coordinator on a big feature film starring Sylvester Stallone (right on the heels of "Rocky") and to be directed by the esteemed Norman Jewison. The movie was called *F.I.S.T.* I knew this was that something big I'd been expecting. When in fact the only thing big about this job was Mr. Stallone's dog, who I was trying to get by air to Dubuque, Iowa, and the star himself told me in a very unagreeable tone of voice that his dog doesn't fly on anything smaller than a 747. That's the day I realized these asshole movie stars figured some little schmuck like me had nothing better to do than to re-route the entire FAA flight plans, or maybe even have a special airstrip put in for their dog. I was going to eat shit for as long as I had to, but then goddamn it, they were going to be working for me someday. For a moment there, Ports was starting to look pretty good again, but I hung in and I guess did an acceptable job because I went on to work for Norman and his producing partner Patrick for the next nine years. Nine years on a Hollywood roller coaster that I swear, "took me places where man had never been before."

THE TALK

(1973-74)

After months of meeting all kinds of women, Dad had gotten pretty discouraged by the results from his ad. Ironically, the woman who had interested him the most, and someone he dated several times, was an amateur ballerina who explained that she only subscribed to *The New York Review of Books* to stay in touch with the alternative point of view. Apparently her politics were extremely rightwing and Dad found her intelligent and contentious enough for a series of good, hearty arguments. I guess that was his idea of a fun date. However, she was not someone he was going to settle down with.

Months went by, during which time he shared no updates with me on his romantic progress. Then suddenly, very much out

105

of the blue, a woman wrote to him from Oxford, where she was just finishing a guest semester teaching theoretical particle physics and was shortly returning to Los Angeles, where she would continue the same work as a permanent faculty member at UCLA. She apologized for answering the ad so late, but she had just picked up a back issue in the Oxford faculty lounge and decided to give it a shot. She explained in the letter about her career, to which she had devoted her adult life, that she was forty-seven years old and had never been married. She also intimated that she was no longer satisfied with this life choice and was trying to take some positive action to change things. She explained that if he were no longer available that he need not even respond and that she would completely understand.

Dad was very taken by her letter and responded immediately and even made a tentative dinner date at La Scala, a very traditional, fancy and romantic restaurant in Beverly Hills that he hoped would be acceptable to her. They met as planned and within three weeks took a trip to France and Italy together and shortly after arriving home decided to share her apartment in Westwood.

He asked if I could help him move the few things he was taking to Nina's on the first available weekend. We packed up his station wagon in Whittier and ended up having to put his

106

mattress on top of the car. Apparently, it was superior in quality to hers, so he was determined to go to the trouble of moving it. The trip, most of which took place on the Santa Monica Freeway, was a good hour plus. My only responsibility along the way was to keep my right hand out the window, planted firmly on the mattress, so that we would know that it remained safely in place to its destination.

Somewhere about halfway to Westwood on the ever-active Santa Monica Freeway Dad abruptly brought up the subject of my sexual persuasion. He gently pointed out that whenever I talked about my future that I never spoke in terms of a relationship or a family and in fact he didn't even know if I was straight or gay or bisexual. I was utterly relieved to have the subject out in the open to be discussed rationally with a man who I sense was not making any judgments, and in fact was trying to make it as easy on me as possible to have "the Talk."

I responded in kind and became very animated in my explanation of my history and my experiences to date (with appropriate discretion) that it must have been fifteen minutes before I realized that both my hands were actively employed inside the car in my enthusiastic communication. It was exactly at that moment that the king size mattress flew off the top of the wagon and caused a seven-car pileup behind us. What a monumental fuck up. We pulled off the freeway, the police arrived and the other drivers, in various stages of outrage, took all the necessary information to make their undoubtedly overstated insurance claims. Remarkably the mattress was still lying in the slow lane, seemingly intact and potentially retrievable. Just as Dad and I were leaning into the traffic to try and rescue it a car came zooming along, drove right over it and carried it off at a zillion miles an hour stuck directly to its underbelly. We both laughed because one couldn't have invented a more absurd scenario. Once again Dad was being a real prince not coming down on me for this debacle because, in fact, it wasn't as clear to me then as it is now, he was so happy to have had "the Talk" even if it was so absurdly truncated by such a comically unsuccessful retrieval of the very object on which he and Nina would soon be having good old-fashioned heterosexual sex. I suppose I might have been more comfortable with a bark-o-lounger interruption but that was not to be and I just had to put embarrassing associations out of my head, apologize for having gotten so distracted by the importance of our communication and move on. The funny thing is that was the end of the discussion. We continued conversing on other subjects until we arrived at Nina's. Dad had made it very clear to me that he was not going to judge me and was only trying to get closer to

108

me and help bring me out. One more sign of his superior and original nature. Of course, I have no idea what he lay thinking later that night on Nina's uncomfortable mattress. We never discussed the subject again.

THE OTHER TALK

I can't actually remember the chronology of the individual talks I had with my parents about my homosexuality. It's my impression that because the one with my mother was when I was still living with Luis, it probably preceded the high-speed freeway disclosure with Dad.

She was recently single and decided impulsively to come to L.A. to visit me after I'd been living there for about a year. Since Luis and I were no longer sharing a bedroom this didn't present any immediate logistical problems. It did, however, involve spending several days with my mother in my new life that I wasn't at all convinced I wished to share with her. I didn't,

111

however, have any good reason to stop her and so we confirmed plans and shortly thereafter I picked her up one evening at Los Angeles International Airport, hoping that the visit would go smoothly.

She told me that she was ravenously hungry upon arriving, so I took her to a Mexican restaurant near the airport rather than driving all the way into Hollywood for dinner. We ordered a pitcher of margaritas and proceeded to get roaring drunk. Mom obviously was going through a lot of life changes, having just divorced her husband after twenty-eight rocky years of marriage, and I sensed that she was more than a little lost. I actually felt sorry for her for the first time in years. Really not since I had witnessed my father hit her when I was about twelve years old and just couldn't believe or accept the brutality of the act, had I felt such pity for her. I had no idea at the time what had occasioned Dad's rage, but I know I implicitly took her side. He was a monster. She was perfect and certainly innocent.

Nothing Mom told me that night fifteen years later was intended to dissuade me of this age-old impression. I wanted desperately to get her off the subject since I was finally developing a very workable, even loving relationship with Dad, and I really didn't want to engage in any more Arthur bashing with her. I had also planned to tell her about me being gay at some point on this visit so if only to change the subject I launched into my story. She cut me off so early into it I'm not sure I got to tell her much of anything. She told me that she had known that I was gay from the time I was twelve or thirteen, when she had found a stack of male physique magazines in my closet (one would have thought that my compulsion to style my little sister's Barbie's hair into a perfect French Twist might have been another clue). She was very upset at the time and consulted with a psychiatrist as to whether I might benefit from therapy of some sort. I laughed when she told me that night that instead of me going to the psychiatrist she ended up in his practice, no doubt dealing with the innumerable problems of hers that had nothing whatsoever to do with me.

Typically, the subject was back to her in record time, given that I had just openly revealed the most important fact of my life to her. She had a real knack for controlling the table, no doubt that's why she had an attic full of bridge trophies. Anyway, she told me that she had a major confession to make as well. About four years into their marriage she had an affair with one of Dad's business partners. Not that I had any right to be, but I was genuinely shocked. I also suddenly recalled that this man who we had grown up calling Uncle Earl was tall, thin, fair-haired and blue-eyed. Oh my god! What was she telling me? I have four siblings, none of whom have my coloring or body type. I think for much deeper reasons I'd spent most of my life feeling as if I were in the wrong family, snatched from the wrong basket at birth, etc. But now to jump a little ahead of my mother and prepare myself for the earth-shattering news that Arthur Milhaupt was not my natural father was even more than the margaritas could prepare me for.

I couldn't be patient and confronted her with my worst fear. She laughed heartily and reassured me that I needn't worry; that was not the point of her story. What she was trying to tell me was that her marriage had been such a disaster from the get go that she consciously chose the one man with whom to have an affair that she assumed would get the biggest rise out of Dad. She said she had only that one purpose in mind and that was to threaten Dad back into loving her. What a concept, I couldn't help thinking. Even Mom admitted in retrospect it was a foolish and desperate measure, especially since the affair was apparently so obvious that finally she knew that Dad must have figured it out and refused to confront her about it. She was finally forced to do the confronting, at which point, with all the arrogance of which he was, I'm sure, capable, Dad reportedly told her to do what she liked, he didn't give a damn. Mom was crushed and ended the affair. She also knew she had played her trump card and probably knew it was all downhill from there. But those were the good old Catholic fifties and they went on to have two more children and another twenty-five years of a highly dysfunctional relationship. When people complain today that marriages don't last like they used to, I always think of my parents and how sad and ultimately irresponsible it was of them to drag out their folly for so long and create and involve so many innocent participants.

So the dinner was drawing to an end and we finally wound our way back to my story. Mom in her inimitable fashion found a way to sum up what was certainly then and probably still is the single most important aspect of my personal development in terms that related to her. As we were getting up from the table, she hugged me and said that actually she was strangely happy about me being gay. I thought it must be the alcohol and didn't really want to hear the rest. But, of course, there was no stopping her. She put her two hands on my cheeks like I was her darling little boy again and said that from the time she accepted this fact about me she comforted herself by knowing that she would always be the number one woman in my life. "Okay Mom, whatever gets you through the night."

CHARLES MILHAUPT

LEAVING UNDER THE INFLUENCE

At some point Jilanne got cut off by her parents. They were intent on her returning to Sydney, where they had promised to buy her a house and set her up in business, but she was equally intent on staying in Los Angeles. So not having any job skills or aspirations, she settled for cocktail waitressing at a series of hip Sunset Strip nightclubs. She had all the right qualifications for the job; good tits and legs. She also liked to sleep until noon, so the hours were perfect. As house mates we were on such opposite schedules we rarely saw each other, which was probably just as well. The harder I worked at following a traditional career path, the sillier Jilanne and all her playgirl behavior seemed to me.

117

I had started to get really tired of the stream of guys through the house and when she and I did intersect there was a palpable, mutual tension growing between us. Things went from bad to worse when she started drinking a lot. I suppose it was an occupational hazard. She lost a number of jobs and had long periods of being out of work altogether. She got a dog and named him Cowboy. He was an adorable Irish Setter puppy, but she was in no position to take on that responsibility. However, she was very attached to him and maybe he was good for her during her decline. There were less and less gentleman callers but she did nab some poor schmoe who had a good job and adored Jilanne. He was around a lot, was a nice enough guy but seriously lacking in the charisma and good looks that had been two previous attributes Jilanne had insisted on in a boyfriend. But beggars can't be choosers and she had literally become a beggar.

One day I came home from work to find Jilanne drunk and on the phone telling our answering service that, "If the kidnappers call about the ransom to be sure and take all the information because she was only going out for a few minutes." They couldn't have been anymore taken aback by this statement than I was. She explained to me in very slurred speech that Cowboy had been kidnapped at the park and that someone had

118

called and said he had her dog and would be calling back about the ransom arrangements. She had apparently sat by the phone for hours drinking the last of her vodka waiting for the call. She was bereft but not so much that she wasn't going to drive down the hill to the liquor store for supplies. Relieved I was home to cover the phone she took off. I immediately called the service to explain that the "kidnapping" involved a dog and that they needn't worry about it as I was home and would take care of it. I'm sure those operators had heard plenty in their time but I just wasn't comfortable leaving them with the impression that they were involved in a real kidnapping. So Jilanne returned, there was a call, and I ended up paying some creep fifty dollars for the return of the poor dog. I refused to involve the police, against Jilanne's demands, since I had this sinking feeling we'd end up in more trouble than the kidnapper once the authorities were involved. Just an example of the kind of paranoia that one develops living with someone capable of anything.

The next disaster occurred when Jilanne talked our friend Bridget, who ironically lived with Richard, Jilanne's "husband," into letting her borrow her car while Bridget was in England visiting her parents for a month. Bridget had never much liked Jilanne, but not knowing what a decline she was in she didn't come up with any good excuse to say no and so reluctantly agreed. I think it was only days later that Jilanne wrapped the car around a telephone pole and was arrested for driving under the influence. This incident drove a deeper wedge between Jilanne and Bridget, especially as Jilanne was rather blasé about the whole thing.

When Jilanne appeared in court to defend herself she tried to explain to the judge that she was perfectly sober at the time of the accident. It was all caused by a freak occurrence of her IUD suddenly coiling inside her and causing her such great pain that she swerved off the road and hit the pole. Apparently, the judge actually laughed and remarked that this was the very first time in his court that a DUI had been argued with an IUD defense. He probably joked to himself that he was dealing with some kind of dyslexic defendant; however, her story didn't fly and she was found guilty, fined and had her license revoked for six months. Her pathetic boyfriend paid the fine and drove her home. Needless to say, Jilanne didn't have the money to have Bridget's car fixed either, so Bridget had to deal with that through her insurance when she got home from England. This might not have been as tense for all of us except that I had agreed to let Bridget stay in our spare room when she returned because she could no longer stand to live with Richard, who had also gone from bad to worse. So I found myself living in a female war zone feeling like I was in some Russ Meyer film, *Return to the Valley of the Echo Park Bitches*. It was hell.

It wasn't long after that Jilanne was out driving her boyfriend's car, without a license, completely drunk, of course, when she hit two young men at the bottom of our hill. Now this was really bad news because they were both badly injured. She was arrested and charged with Felony Drunk Driving and faced possible imprisonment this time because of the seriousness of her crime and her recent record. The trial was to take place shortly and she was out on a reasonably large amount of bail put up by you-know-who.

We were all appalled and disgusted with her and couldn't conjure up much in the way of sympathy. She made up her addled mind without telling us or her poor, misguided boyfriend (whose car was totaled, by the way) that she was going to skip the country, forfeit his bail money and accept the fact that she could never come back to America. It was one way to get rid of a bad roommate.

Bridget was the happiest of all because she could share the house with just me living in a more commodious room and never have to lay eyes on Jilanne again. I certainly wasn't sorry to see Jilanne go, but I'd had quite a different history with her, and I did have pangs of sadness from watching a person, with whom

121

I'd once been in love, degenerate so dramatically that at the end she was unrecognizable. One more example of the miracle of alcohol, I suppose.

About five years later, having never heard anything from or about Jilanne, Bridget and I received a Christmas card from her. We opened it together and burst out laughing. It was a photo of Jilanne seated on a big yacht, naked from the waist up, looking marvelous with those famous tits back in shape. She was holding a glass of champagne in toasting fashion and the card simply read, "Cheers." In that photo, with that pose, cheers clearly meant "fuck you" in Australian.

JUSTICE FOR SOME

(1978-79)

Jewison and Palmer's next production was ...*And Justice for All*, starring Al Pacino. Frankly Jewison had virtually no reason to have even noticed me on the previous film, but his producer was apparently impressed with my organizational skills and willingness to work hard. He felt I'd learned enough about running a production office to promote me to Production Coordinator on the new film. That was a really big deal for me and a giant leap of responsibility. Traditionally Production Coordinators are, first of all women and secondly known for being thoroughly overworked and underpaid to the point that if they stick it out long enough they very often become bitter or alcoholic or both and just generally dysfunctional. I think Patrick

123

was taking a big chance on me, but at the same time he was getting fresh meat and someone he could control, an ideal fit for his particular management style. I can't do him justice with any brief description because he was a very complex, highly screwed up individual who had worked his way up the Hollywood system starting as a day laborer at one of the old studios. By the time I appeared in his career he was a full producer and business partner of one of Hollywood's most consistently successful directors. Having held jobs at so many levels of the production side of movie making, he had an enormous amount of knowledge and could smell a bad job being done from miles away. He thrived on the reputation of being a tough guy and definitely played bad cop to Norman's good cop in numerable high-level situations. The irony was that he wasn't such a bad guy if you worked hard, were committed and didn't bullshit him. Norman on the other hand was a born charmer. A Boy Wonder in early TV in his native Toronto, he had had an early and fantastic success as a feature film director in Hollywood, decades before the birth of the "baby moguls."

One of the best stories Norman ever told me about his early days was when he was making the transition from television to film and Judy Garland was virtually begging him to film her televised comeback concert at Carnegie Hall. He kept declining the offer, and she kept insisting. Finally he went to see her in concert in New Jersey shortly before the New York concert engagement was to take place, planning to see her show, go back stage and politely turn down the job in person. Well, shortly after she received him in her dressing room she was interrupted by an assistant with a phone call that she had to take (in front of Norman). As he tells it, she greeted the caller quite intimately, told him it was much too late for him to be calling and then said, "Oh Jack, I have someone here with me and I really don't think I can." Then she giggled, put her hand over the receiver and mouthed the words "the President" to Norman. She continued the conversation, "Well okay, but just a little of it," at which point she sang the several key phrases from "Somewhere over the Rainbow." She asked the President to give her love to Jackie and hung up. Who knows if there was anyone on the other end of that line, but Norman was hooked. As a dyed-in-the-wool Democrat and a huge admirer of President Kennedy, I think it was all too much for this kid from Canada. He committed then and there to the show and went on to direct an Emmy winning masterpiece that truly led to her comeback in the form of her short-lived weekly series, several episodes of which were directed by Norman as well. The unhappy ending to this period of his career was that she was really spiraling downwards and becoming more and more dependent on Norman. Middle of the

125

night suicide calls were a regular occasion, and he had to get out of this sick and insoluble situation and get back to his conquest of Hollywood. Whenever he talks about this time I can tell it made him really sad even though by the time I knew him he was no longer a man I could picture having such feelings. Too many years of crazy stars, difficult studio executives and over-the-top personal ego gratification had turned him into a different person.

The picture was shot in Baltimore for three months with an additional three weeks of studio work to be done in L.A. at the end. As a complete novice to the job I had the good fortune of working directly for a fantastic Production Manager named Larry De Way, whose experience and professionalism made my job relatively easy. Also he had worked with Norman and Patrick on several previous films, which was a great help to me in winding my way through their idiosyncrasies with his guidance. On top of everything, Larry was very generous about my lack of experience and was amazingly patient about teaching me my job, although he had plenty to do himself.

Every day presented new and sometimes very unlikely challenges. I remember one incident when the shooting company was miles out of town at a small private airport where a scene was to be shot with Al and Jack Warden eating cherry pie in the airport coffee shop. Well, everything was there; twelve trucks of

126

equipment, three mobile homes for the stars and director, enough electrical cable to stretch from New York to L.A., a crew of ninety professionals, but no cherry pie. I got a panic call from Larry that I was to charter a helicopter, buy three cherry pies and get them out there ASAP. I was starting to understand why movies were so expensive.

One of my main responsibilities, aside from baby-sitting an endless amount of spoiled brat cast and crew members, was to arrange all the travel involved with the movie. Our schedule was a killer in this regard, as we were to finish shooting in Baltimore on the day before Christmas Eve, give everyone a ten-day hiatus, and then reassemble in Los Angeles to start the stage work after New Years. This was largely Norman's idea, since he wanted to have a decent holiday himself, and it made him look like a hero to the crew. However, it left me and my overworked travel agent with the task of sending ninety people off in nearly ninety different directions on one of the busiest travel days of the year. It was especially crazy-making, as nobody could seem to make up their feeble minds where they wanted to go.

Just to make the cheese more binding we were shooting the climactic courtroom scene that was written for Al's character to let loose with the ultimate crowd-pleasing performance on the final three days in Baltimore. Al had a different idea and thought the scene should be underplayed and somehow that was going to make it more powerful. He and Norman argued vociferously for days before the sequence was to be filmed. Ultimately Al got his way, the big scene was finally completed, and we wrapped with everyone planning to scatter out of Baltimore the next day. Al came to Norman's office late that night and confessed that he had decided he was wrong, and that they needed to reshoot the whole sequence the way Norman had intended. Norman was furious and I was on the verge of a nervous breakdown listening through the door with the travel agent on hold in case we were going to stay and shoot another three days (over Christmas!). Norman solved the problem by promising Al that when they got back to the studio they would cut the scene together, and if it, in fact, didn't work we would come back to Baltimore after the studio work was completed and reshoot it. I knew Norman was just buying time and wasn't giving up his holiday for some neurotic actor, but it did the trick and we all left as planned.

I got home late on Christmas Eve, exhausted and not exactly imbued with the holiday spirit. Bridget was sick with a bad flu and our friend Christine was visiting from London. When I woke up the next morning and Bridget was feeling no better, I called the ten people she had invited to Christmas dinner and canceled it. It took me an hour or so to realize just what I'd done. Ten people, our closest friends, suddenly had no Christmas plans thanks to me. I called all of them back and apologized for my thoughtlessness and said they should certainly come, but that as Bridget was the cook in the house it might be a little on the informal side. We had a huge turkey that had been thawed, half cooked until I canceled dinner and then re-frozen and we decided that it had the potential for being very unhealthy at best. Christine sweetly offered to make bangers and mash so that our guests could have an English Christmas, be it ever so humble. Actually Bridget came back to life enough to receive our guests as they arrived and make a joke out of my previously having canceled Christmas on them. Then our friend Susan arrived, looking a bit like she'd just made a rough crossing of the English Channel. Susan always had her own odd way about her, but she was really reeling as she stumbled into the living room announcing that there was a dead body in the road. I dismissed her statement and suggested she have a drink and calm down. But she wouldn't let up and said her very sober, lawyer boyfriend David was back on the road checking out the situation. We lived at the end of a very long unmarked dirt road in a remote part of Echo Park on the east side of L.A. I got a flashlight, muttering something about it being a pile of firewood and went down to see for myself. Sure enough, I found David crouched over a very

129

dead, naked body of a fiftyish, male Chicano whose throat had been slashed.

I ran back to the house and confirmed Susan's story and told Bridget that there were gallons of blood on the road. To which she responded in her inimitably British fashion, "Don't be daft, Charlie, the human body doesn't contain gallons of blood." Christine kept insisting we drag the poor man into the house for bangers and mash, and I called the police. None of us had ever seen so many cop cars in one place. The police theorized that he was the victim of a gang murder, and that our driveway had been mistaken for an unused road, and the culprits probably figured it might be weeks before the body would be discovered. We felt it was prudent to keep Susan out of the official procedures, so David and I shared the endless task of answering the same questions, over and over, as the detectives and investigators kept arriving. Finally everyone had gone home, I'd gone to bed and at about three in the morning there was another bang on the door. Bridget got up and I heard her tell two new policeman who had not yet gotten in on the act that "Mr. Milhaupt has retired for the evening. He's had quite enough of this affair for one night, and I suggest if you wish to speak to him that you return in the morning." It sounded from their non-responsiveness that she then just closed the door on their no doubt astonished faces and went back to bed. She made an excellent guard dog throughout the many years we lived together, but this was her *piece de resistance*.

The company reassembled after the holidays for the three weeks of studio work. I had the best "What did you do over the holidays?" story. Before we had completed the work in L.A., Norman lived up to his promise of cutting together the infamous scene and everyone agreed Al was right. It was going to have to be reshot. Once we'd finished in L.A. a skeleton crew went back to Baltimore and shot the scene as it was originally intended. Ironically I think it's that scene that garnered a Best Actor Oscar nomination for Al, since the rest of the picture was flawed at best.

From here on in I remained on staff with Jewison and Palmer, essentially getting a promotion on every new picture. Each film was a totally unique experience and the economic stability of staying with them for nine years was very appealing. It did, however, hold me back in an industry that thrived on disloyalty and upward mobility. I think I knew from the very beginning that I didn't have the killer instinct to carve out a career in such a competitive back-stabbing business, so I just stayed put and slowly learned a lot from the two of them, even if it was at the expense of plenty of mistreatment and outright

131

abuse. Nobody ever said it was going to be easy, we all know that.

But what I didn't know was that nobody there ever said anything because the industry was like a private club and even your "closest" colleagues would do anything to keep you from becoming a member. Lovely place, that Hollywood.

TOUGH LOVE

(1981)

Luis and I had not completely lost contact, certainly less so as I seemed to be finding some success in the movie business. I was apparently on his famous list of "the five hundred." Those were the people he called weekly to ask, "How are you? What are you doing? Oh how wonderful." It's hard not to hear it with his intonation that stretched the words out in a sing song way that was exactly the same every time that underscored the rhetorical aspect of his inquiries. But nevertheless, it was meant to be an

133

honor to be on the list so fill him in I would. It occurred to him at one point that I should meet a friend of his who had gone to

Harvard (well after Luis had, but you know how those Ivy Leaguers stick together). Luis took me to a wonderful old Hollywood apartment complex that turned out to have been owned by Cecil B. de Mille (a home without a star provenance was hardly worth living in Hollywood). The man I was to meet lived in one of those chairman units straight out of the twenties. His name was Gregg and I think the occasion was a small dinner party.

Being so gregarious by nature, it was hard for me to tell what if any impact I made on Gregg as he was nearly silent the entire evening. Somehow we made contact shortly thereafter and made a plan to go to a private press screening of a soon to be released movie. Gregg was an entertainment staff writer at the *L.A. Times* and received innumerable such invitations for two. I was Delighted to be asked; I think it was probably my first such opportunity. We continued to do things of that sort over the next year and spent an enormous amount of time together. We also talked nearly daily on the phone. From my point of view, even though Gregg was gay, there was never any question that we were anything but just friends. Apparently the same did not hold true for Gregg. The night we attended the Golden Globes

Awards together everything was made eminently clear to me. The evening was a black tie, star-studded event and really a lot of fun. I suppose it was gutsy of him to take a male date, but we were living in the post-Stonewall, pre-AIDS honeymoon of gay liberation then.

When we got back to Gregg's house where my car was parked I thanked him for taking me to such a big event and started to get into my car when he asked me in for a drink. I didn't really feel like it, having had plenty at the event, because unlike the Oscars, the Golden Globes is one, big, silly dinner party and nearly everyone gets sloshed. He pressed and I acquiesced.

We got inside, looking very sophisticated (I thought) in our rented tuxedos, Gregg poured some drinks and proceeded to tell me that he wanted to have sex with me and had wanted to for the year or so we'd been friends. I was flabbergasted. There had never been a hint from him of his attraction to me. I kind of understood why however, since he was someone who had a very hard time expressing himself directly in any real issues. Gregg existed on the edge of a conversation coming up with the wicked one-liner that would bring the house down. There was also no question that he had an incredibly low opinion of himself in the looks department. Partly this was a valid assessment. He was not

135

terribly attractive. But he was funny and smart and until this evening had seemed like my best friend.

When I resisted he actually argued the point as if it had been planned. He told me that for some time now he'd been taking me to events to which I would otherwise have had no entree. He was certainly right about that, but I guess I'd have thought that my company had been adequate compensation, if such a deal is necessary between friends. He continued by saying that this evening's event was especially generous of him to have shared with me and that it was the least I could do to return the favor and sleep with him. I was really lost. I wasn't angry but I wasn't interested in having sex with my best friend just because I'd gotten to see a bunch of movie stars in person who I could have seen on TV at home with no ransom held over my head. He was clearly determined and I imagine very drunk. I was pretty sober, but decided that I would try to cooperate so as to not hurt his feelings terribly and somehow just get through it. I certainly didn't see it as the beginning of a hot and heavy love affair. It was a payback to a friend who probably needed love and affection more than sex anyway. Although, that I could have been wrong about.

The lack of enthusiasm and interest with which I undressed upstairs in his bedroom didn't seem to put him off. I guess having made the big step nothing was going to deter him. We got into bed naked and tried a little kissing which felt completely weird to me. Then he started sucking my cock and I wasn't getting an erection. That was not a good sign. In fact I think that's when I pulled away and said this was not going to work, I was sorry but sex between us was just not in the cards. I can't really remember Gregg's reaction. He probably had such mixed feelings of anger and embarrassment that nothing clear was communicated. I got dressed in a deadly silence, said goodnight and let myself out.

Miraculously, without ever discussing the incident, he and I went on to be the closest of friends for a good ten years. In fact, he and Bridget and I became a sort of triangulated family of orphans, three people who needed nobody, but couldn't get along without each other on a daily basis.

BEST FRIENDS

(1981-82)

Norman's next film was a romantic comedy entitled *Best Friends*, written by Barry Levinson and Valerie Curtin, who had also written ...*and Justice for All*. It was an autobiographical story about the two of them deciding to get married after successfully living and working together as Hollywood screenwriters for several years. Their idea for a honeymoon was to go from Los Angeles by train to Buffalo to visit her parents first, whom he had never met and then to Baltimore to visit his parents, whom she had never met. The concept being that each visit reduces the adult newlywed to a child again and the relationship falls apart and the marriage seems like a disastrous mistake until the

139

inevitable happy ending back in Hollywood. It was unusually light material for Norman to take on at this point in his career, and he was quite ambivalent about it. Actually, I had developed enough influence with him by then that I was partly responsible for talking him into doing it. However, I had very specific casting ideas that were paramount to my enthusiasm for the project.

There was never any question about who was going to play the female lead because Goldie Hawn had been given the script very early on, loved it, and committed right away. She was perfect for the role and none of us, especially the studio paying for it, could have been happier. The big question was who was going to star opposite her. There was a general consensus that he had to be a star of her caliber or the balance would be thrown off. The cast budget seemed to be of little consequence, as the studio was so optimistic about the commercial appeal of this project and Goldie was still very hot from "Private Benjamin." Since the idea was based on the ethnic contrast between the characters that reflected Barry and Valerie, we first thought of Dustin Hoffman. He turned it down. More lists were compiled with all the usual suspects by the highly overpaid and useless casting director. I happened to have just seen Kevin Kline in New York in the Shakespeare In the Park production of "The Pirates of Penzance." He was extraordinary and received unilateral raves from the critics. It was a career-making roll. I assume Alan Pakula cast him in "Sophie's Choice" having at least heard about the performance if he hadn't actually seen it himself. Anyway, I went out on a limb and made my big pitch to Norman and Patrick that he would be perfect for the roll even if he wasn't a big star. No go. Norman sent the script to Burt Reynolds who accepted the part the next day and that was it. We had the marquee value the studio was looking for, but we had an actor who refused to play the part as written: Jewish from Baltimore. We also had ourselves a man who got five million dollars for being attractive, tall, funny and hirsute, none of which were exactly the case. The number of wigs that he wore in the picture were, for example, incalculable and of course they were never to be mentioned. I remember mornings when Norman would whisper to me near the camera, "Look what he's got on today. How the hell am I going to make any of this match?"

Goldie and I literally fell in love with each other on sight. It didn't hurt that we were born on the same day, but it was a lot more than that. She was the most open-hearted, infectiously funny person I'd ever met. The connection was so strong that it was enough to make me believe in past life connections. On the other hand, Burt seemed to take an instant dislike to me, openly resented my presence in script meetings with the writers and never once talked to me in the months it took to make the film. I always theorized that it had something to do with me being gay and his own personal issue in that department. Whatever his problem was it didn't make my job any easier or pleasant, and I eventually just gave up on him and pretended, as he did with me, that he just wasn't there whenever we were in the same room, which was often. His publicist was my saving grace because he was a wonderful character with whom I made fast friends, and he never stopped entertaining me with hilarious old Hollywood war stories. He also tried to explain away Burt's weirdness as best he could which was after all, part of his job, but the closer we got the more dish I'd get from him on Burt and his bizarre entourage.

So poor Valerie and Barry had to quickly rewrite Burt's character to take out the Jewishness, which of course robbed the story of its validity and completely weakened the comic conflict inherent to the original story. His "family" was relocated to Virginia and drained of any recognizable ethnicity and the story lost its punch. Even the stuff in Buffalo with Goldie's WASPy parents didn't work because once again it lacked conflict. The big joke in reality is that Goldie is Jewish and god only knows what Burt might be, but the difference is she's an actor playing a part and he's Burt Reynolds still living off that Cosmo spread that turned out to be a brilliant career move.

We went back to L.A. to finish the movie on the stage and now we're months into the schedule and Burt has still never acknowledged my existence. One morning he calls for his publicist to come to his famous blue bus in which he and his flunkies hang out. It was so unusual for Burt to ask for Stanley that early in the day he couldn't help but wonder what was up. He found Burt lying down in the back of the bus. Burt proceeded to ask him two or three totally banal and unnecessary questions that any number of the guys in the bus could have answered, after which Stanley said if that was all, he had to get back to his office to do some work. Burt let him go but stopped him at the last moment and asked, "Is it true that Charlie Milhaupt lives with Bridget Byrne?" Stanley couldn't wait to report this to me as he knew of our problems and even he was fascinated by Burt's sudden interest in me. Well, it turns out that several years before at some press junket for Burt, Bridget, who was an entertainment journalist, was mistaken by Burt as Joyce Haber who was a famous, drunken columnist for the *L.A. Times* who had recently printed something nasty about him in the paper. He let loose at Bridget with a string of expletives and near threats (he's famous for being wildly paranoid about the media) that left Bridget speechless (a rare occurrence). His other full-time publicist was there and rushed over to intervene, took Bridget aside and explained that Burt was hypoglycemic and that his blood sugar must have suddenly dropped. Bridget, bless her soul, said in a voice loud enough for Burt to hear "If the man is ill he should be in an institution." Apparently, Burt never got over it and managed to hold it against even me years later. How the fuck do these people even tie their own shoes in the morning? Maybe Burt Reynolds wears slip-ons.

This poor movie was hexed from the beginning. One of the final elements involved in making a movie is the recording of the music score. I always found it hard to understand that by the time the film makers got to the recording studio there was usually a maximum of two, maybe three days scheduled for what can often be such an important aspect of a film. Like everything else on a film it's, big surprise, about money. On top of it, by then there's not a hell of a lot a director and producer can do about the results because they've been busy making a movie while the composer has been independently busy composing a score. I think it was the architect Phillip Johnson who said that "Talking about music is like dancing about architecture." In other words there's not much one can do to revise the work on the spot if you are unhappy. Of course, sometimes a whole score is thrown out, and they start from scratch with a new composer. That would generally be a prohibitively expensive and desperate measure.

Norman had hired one of the greats, Michel LeGrande, to score the film. They had worked together previously, and Norman liked to use big names whenever possible. When the day came to record the music and there were close to four hundred musicians assembled, Michel was rushed to the hospital with a kidney stone. He was in unbearable pain but insisted on being given a shitload of morphine and reported late for the scoring session. There was no question whatsoever that the moribund quality of the music to underscore this light, romantic comedy was largely a side-effect of the morphine. It struck one as an appropriate soundtrack for "Death in Venice."

The next and last disaster on *Best Friends* was mine. I had stupidly told Norman at some point that I was very friendly with Pauline Kael, the Grande Dame of film critics. He asked if I would take a print to New York and show it to her privately, somehow influence the most single-minded critic of her time, and wind up with a good review in *The New Yorker*. Norman also knew that a very small number of people read *The New Yorker*, but that Pauline had at least a dozen followers in the field who would parrot her opinions on this film. It was all up to me. The screening was arranged. Pauline brought a few friends and

145

greeted me very warmly. I remember it was winter because at the end of the screening Pauline was busy buttoning up her fur coat to head out into the cold when she said to me, "Well Charlie, are you going to slit your wrists now or are you going to wait until the picture comes out?" We parted ways and my heart was pounding because Norman was at his farm in Toronto waiting for my phone call with the results of the screening. I had to call him. All I could think to say was that she was not very committal on the subject and wasn't sure when she was going to write the review. He wasn't happy but at least he didn't have to hear the truth. That was my job.

ISLAND FEVER

(1982)

The summer after *Best Friends* was made, Goldie invited me to come and stay with her in Ibiza, a Spanish Island off the coast of Barcelona. At that time it was a watering hole for the beautiful young international set and she had rented what they call a *finca* (little house) there for the summer that she was sharing with her then boyfriend, an out of work French actor named Yves and her two young children from her previous marriage, an adorable boy and girl ages five and three. The house was a beautiful, simple white structure situated on a hillside covered with olive trees. She had a couple other friends visiting from L.A., so when I arrived we were quite a houseful.

Our days were spent going to the beach, where we would eat wonderful local food at funky little stands under thatched roofs, taking siestas back at home and going out to dinner or cooking big family dinners at home. It was all very simple and everyone got on famously. That is with the exception of Yves, who was often what my mother used to call a real pill. He was clearly full of resentment that Goldie was so successful, and he wasn't. Somehow she managed to keep peace most of the time, but I know I wouldn't have put up with his arrogant, chauvinistic bullshit for a minute. However, I'd long since given up on understanding what keeps people together and as I was hardly an expert on the subject, I did my best to stay out of it.

My stay was drawing to an end and Goldie had planned a big dinner at a restaurant in the middle of the island that was supposed to be great. It was quite a drive and by the time we all got there it was pitch black. Goldie realized she had left her daughter's bottle at home and that we'd never get through the evening without it, and what with Yves being such a gentleman, Goldie had to drive back to retrieve it herself. She left her daughter in my care, as well as her big fat wallet, which for some reason she took out of her purse before she left. I suppose she thought Yves might order a drink and not be able to pay for it. When she returned we all went to the big table, had a great dinner and raucous fun and then the bill arrived. Goldie insisted on paying and ever so casually asked me for her wallet. I didn't have it. I made a weak argument that she'd never given it to me, hoping like hell I was right and that it was back at the house. In my gut, however, I knew that I had somehow managed to lose it. The rest of us pitched in and paid the bill and we raced home in a very tense car. Yves was a big help as usual because he was drunk and he kept saying that this would teach her a good lesson. It will be good for her to have no money because she thought money was everything. Easy to say when you're being supported by an overly generous woman all summer long in one of the world's trendiest resorts. I wanted to strangle him because I could feel Goldie's temples throbbing with anger as we approached the house. The thing was, she had not only been to the bank that day and gotten an enormous amount of cash, but the wallet contained all of her credit cards and identification as well. I wanted to shrivel up and die when it was nowhere to be found in the house. Goldie immediately called her agent in L.A., explained the situation and went off to bed. I was leaving the next day (thank god) and had about a hundred dollars left to get me to New York, where I was spending a week with friends on Fire Island (yet another island I'd never visited). I had planned it so that I could cash a check there and would be okay for the rest of my vacation.

The next morning Goldie had calmed down a little and asked if I wanted to go get a coffee at the nearby, dusty little town. Of course it would have to be my treat. I felt compelled to give her as much of my cash as I could possibly spare so I left myself with twenty dollars and gave her the rest. I was praying the William Morris Agency was going to come through for one of their top clients and somehow this meager offering would carry her through. As we sat dejectedly at a little table in the dirt outside of this bar that belonged in a spaghetti western, a mere twelve hours after her call had been made to L.A., a funky old car pulled up, and a man in a bowler hat got out and walked over to us with a brown paper bag in his hand. He stood timidly in front of us and said to Goldie, "Miss Goldie Hawn?" To which she said "Yes," at which point he deposited the bag on the table saying it was from Mr. Stan Kamen (her agent in L.A.) and got back in his car and drove away. Goldie opened the bag and broke out laughing. It was five thousand dollars in cash. Boy, sometimes being a movie star can really be an asset. Of course there was still the issue of her missing ID, but somehow the money took the edge off the crisis. I felt so badly about the whole thing that I didn't have the courage to ask for my eighty dollars back and it probably never occurred to her.

My flight from Ibiza to Barcelona was at eight o'clock the next morning and it was Yves' bright idea that we should stay up all night disco hopping (a common activity at the time on that island) and then he and Goldie would drive me straight to the airport. Well we made it until about six in the morning in a series of comparably wild nightspots before they wanted to go home and go to bed. Their parting words to me were that I could leave the car at the airport with the keys under the mat and they would find it later. Oh, fine. I had no fucking idea where the airport was, and I'd been up all night and I was a wreck and a half. I managed, however, and got on the plane to Barcelona from where I thought for some reason I was flying directly to New York. I settled in for a long sleep and the next thing I knew I was being shaken awake by an Iberia Airlines stewardess, as I was the only passenger left on the plane that had landed and was unloading on the tarmac into a bus to the terminal. I was not a popular passenger as I stumbled down the stairs to a bus full of Spaniards who had been kept waiting by me in unbearable heat for god knows how long. It wasn't until we got to the terminal that I discovered we were in Madrid, where I was changing planes for New York. I blamed it on Yves because one thing I've never been is a flake.

I got to New York, where my friends had instructed me to look for a jitney to a place on Long Island called Sayville, where I was to get on a ferry that would take me to Fire Island Pines and then get on a water taxi to go up the island to a community called Water Island where they were staying. By the time I got to Water Island, I felt as if I had crossed half the world on nearly every conceivable form of transportation. I was also dragging along too much luggage and suffering from severe jet lag. The little speed boat no sooner arrived at Water Island than my friends, a group of about six or seven wildly vacationing guys came running down the dock screaming that I should hold the taxi and just throw my stuff in the house, grab a sweater and come back because we were going down island to a dinner party. The house we were invited to was in a tiny community called Oaklyville and was not accessible by boat in low tide, which apparently we were in. The taxi driver was a local Long Island boy who had to put up with groups of this sort all summer, and I think got kind of a kick out of telling us that when he got near Oaklyville, about five hundred yards out into the pitch black bay, that that was as close as he could take the boat. There were one or two lights on in the few houses on the shore, otherwise there was no sign of any sort where we were headed. He suggested we take off our pants, as the water was probably waist high and we were going to have to wade in. I did as he suggested and got out of the boat first, only to find that the water was neck high. Everyone else got out of the boat, he sped away and we were standing up to our heads in the bay paralyzed by uncontrollable giggles and not moving anywhere. Finally we came more or less to our senses and started toward the shore, still bursting into wild laughter at how silly this all was. We finally reached the beach, found the house, which was closed up, dark and apparently empty. It was most unfortunately the wrong night and our hosts were not home. I was no longer amused. We had to walk five miles up the ocean side of the island to the next community just to be able to call another taxi to get us home, and we were soaked to the gills. When we got to Cherry Grove my companions insisted on staying there and dancing at the disco and making a night of it. I think by then it had been about thirty hours since I'd been in a bed and I remember just sitting on the dock and bursting into tears and saying over and over again to myself, "I hate this island, I hate this island." Everything was better after a good night's sleep, and I've since rented my own summer houses on Water Island several times. It's a very magical place. I just became a little more careful about confirming dinner invitations.

G.R.I.D.

(1984)

It was one night during that same week on water island that our household was invited next door for a dinner party. That night our host was home and expecting us. There were about twelve men ranging in ages from early twenties to mid-forties. I imagine most of us had been engaging in reasonably promiscuous sexual activity for some time, as it was the era for such behavior. The bath houses and sex clubs in the big cities were overflowing with customers and tons of anonymous sex had been the going thing in the bushes on that very island for years.

One of the dinner guests was a man we called Doctor Bob. He was a doctor who was generous with the contents of his

155

medical bag and therefore a very popular guest. He was also a good-looking and charming guy. That night he was serious however. At his suggestion, after dinner, we all collected in the kitchen so that he could fill us in on a strange new medical phenomenon that had appeared in the gay community. There were apparently an increasing number of gay men being admitted to urban hospitals with something the papers were calling Gay Cancer. Tough men who otherwise should have been quite hearty were suddenly dying of inexplicable infections. Most of the cases were diagnosed to be a kind of viral pneumonia normally seen in advanced cancer patients whose immune system had given out on them. There were not a huge number of cases yet but there was a pattern forming and there was a definite theory that this was a gay disease connected somehow to the highly promiscuous behavior of the day.

The situation was grave enough that the disease quickly took on a more scientific name. It was called G.R.I.D., standing for Gay Related Immuno Deficiency. Doctor Bob had us all enthralled in his horror story. The problem was that there was such a shortage of information at this point that it was as if we were little boys at camp and our counselor was telling us scary stories and then sending us off to bed afraid of the dark.

The one practical piece of advice he was able to share with us was that we would be well advised to discreetly check any future sexual partners for swollen glands in various parts of the body. He used me as an example and showed the captive audience of speechless men how to appear to be engaged in gentle foreplay, running one's exploring hands over a body and carefully checking key areas; in the neck, under the arms, in the groin. His advice was that a clear indication of swollen glands would be a sign to back off and disengage from any sexual encounter. Strangely this was even before there was an understanding that this was definitely a sexually transmitted disease. It's just that correct assumptions were being made by the medical community that there must be a connection. I think that this was also the time when poppers (amyl nitrate) were thought to be a key component of the budding "plague." He warned us against their use that night as well just as the "lecture" broke up.

Ironically, moments later, Doctor Bob came to me with his famous black bag and asked me, "if I wanted to go up or down?" Honestly, I'd never heard that question except in bad movies about hippies made by Roger Corman, but of course I was in heaven. Since there was a guest there with whom I had shared an immediate sexual attraction, I answered "down" (much better for sex in my case), and he proceeded to get me completely loaded

157

on some controlled substance. I quickly ended up in bed back at my house with this total stranger, having what we later came to understand was completely unsafe sex. That subject had not been included in the lesson, as it was well before anyone knew how the virus was transmitted. Wouldn't it be ironic if I were first exposed to HIV that very night. Who knows? Who cares at this point? I think I'm just such an irony addict that sometimes I like to revel in that possibility even though the odds are that it could have been earlier, later and certainly with any number of other partners with whom I didn't know any better but to engage in unprotected sex. Frankly I almost never think about any of this because it's such a moot point. But for me the BIG CHANGE started that night with Doctor Bob. At least seventy-five percent of the men who were there that night have since died of AIDS and I'm still here telling my story, and I hope theirs as well.

THE *ICEMAN* COMETH, UNFORTUNATELY

(1984)

Norman received a script from a young, Canadian neophyte screenwriter entitled *Iceman* that was in such rough form that none of us could believe that he was even interested. It was at least one hundred and eighty-five pages long and not written in anything close to traditional screenplay format. But it contained the seed of an idea that appealed to Jewison, so Patrick and I were asked to read it and advise him on what we should do.

The gist of the story was that a group of scientists are in the extreme Arctic in an elaborate outpost built to study the local ecology (for no reason, as written) and they discover an ancient block of ice that contains a perfectly preserved Neanderthal man.

159

To make a much too long story shorter, the ice is melted, the man comes back to life and develops a relationship with the lead archeologist. There ensues a struggle over his destiny as this discovery is so earth-shattering (sound familiar to any King Kong fans?) and he is ultimately set free by his "friend," the young anthropologist, and presumably returns back into the ice from which he came. Fortunately Norman had the sense not to direct this material himself and hired the Australian director Fred Schepisi for the task. I thought that was a great idea, as I had liked his previous films, *The Legend of Jimmy Blacksmith* in particular, and felt that he might be able to make something artful out of this derivative nonsense. The studio approved of him, having worked with him once previously and so he "came aboard" as they love to say in Hollywood, as if we are all working on a ship, and set right to work with the writer crafting something workable out of the original mess.

While all of this was taking place, Patrick came to me and announced that I was going to be made the Associate Producer of the film. This was such a big leap in credit if not responsibility (as Patrick never really let me really do anything of any consequence anyway) that I honestly didn't know how to react. I remember going home that night and having dinner with Gregg and Bridget and saying that I was going to turn down the offer because I hated the project, I didn't believe that the important title was anything but titular, which embarrassed me, and I didn't have any relationship with Fred and didn't want him to feel saddled with one more useless "suit." Gregg, in typical fashion, took a long drag on his cigarette and said I should go on, "That's Incredible," meaning in the movie industry it is absolutely unheard of to turn down promotions, especially one of this sort that would propel my name onto the front edits of the eventual feature film and have the potential of increasing my currency in the industry-at-large incalculably. I knew he was right, but I also sensed some kind of real trouble ahead on this project. Frankly, I didn't even have much say on the issue, since to turn down the offer would have been tantamount to quitting, which I was less prepared to do than to move up the shaky ladder.

So suddenly Fred had an Associate Producer who was assigned originally to help with the development of the script, a known talent of mine in the company. However, I was working with two people who did not get along in the least, and Fred had very definite ideas about what he wanted to do with the project. He quickly got rid of the writer and proceeded to rewrite the script himself. He insisted I find an expert on Neanderthal "language" to help him lend authenticity to the dialogue. Of

161

course, there was no such thing as Neanderthal language as far as anyone knows, but I did find a professor at Harvard who had spent years theorizing on what their language might have been, based on the skeletal remains from that period. He was brought to L.A. and worked with us for weeks creating sounds for the *Iceman* character with which Fred was satisfied. Norman and Pat thought we'd gone off the deep end and, I'm sure, started to regret the relationship they had created between me and the director. Pat did his best to run interference, which, as usual, made everything more difficult. In the end, however, we had a script that made vague sense and appealed to Fred because it contained more of a mystical quality and considerably more scientific verisimilitude than had originally been the case.

Then the studio intervened in the casting, a key issue for them as always. They were intent on Timothy Hutton playing the anthropologist even though he was all of twenty-two years old. He was, however, still potentially big box office, since it hadn't been long since he'd won his Best Supporting Actor Oscar for his role in *Ordinary People*. It was of course a ridiculous premise that a character of his age would have the education and experience to have such a prestigious job in this already illogical outpost. But since logic was not the mainstay of this project from the beginning, Fred accepted the mandate (unhappily) and

162

proceeded to concentrate on who would play the important title role. Fortunately the studio felt they had their protection with Hutton so that we could go with an unknown for the Neanderthal.

The casting director was a wild and funny and quite talented woman named Mary Goldberg. She and I hit it off, at least in the beginning, and were often reduced to very unprofessional fits of giggles when we found ourselves having to ask non-actors that Fred had met in an airport or seen on the street somewhere to strip down to their underwear and jump around the room, on desk tops, couches and windowsills while we videotaped them for Fred and Norman. The more of this time we wasted the clearer it became to us and even Fred that we needed a real actor for the role. Mary had seen an exceptional man on stage in New York named John Lone, who had starred in an off-Broadway play he had written and directed. After a completely useless open call in New York we finally met John, and Fred was almost instantly convinced he'd found his Iceman. It was a real triumph for Mary and once Norman and the studio were sold on the idea we brought him out to L.A. for physical fitness training and language classes with our nutty professor. It's funny for me to think now that the man who later played the glamorous lead in

The Last Emperor was the same young man I would drop off at the Motel 6 in Culver City every night after work.

The rest of the casting was pretty routine and we ended up with a respectable group of actors, including Danny Glover in his first movie role. It was at this point, however, that I was really starting to have personal trouble being stuck between a rock (Fred) and a hard place (Patrick). It seemed that everything Fred did annoyed the shit out of Patrick, and it was apparently my job to straighten him out. That was ridiculous, as Fred was a very strong, confident and original film maker, and they had gotten what they asked for. But the tension started to make every day of work miserable. This was while we were still in pre-production on top of it and hadn't yet set off with a huge crew to the frozen Arctic in February, where we were going to work outdoors in temperatures as low as fifty degrees below zero.

Things got so bad for me that I slipped into a near suicidal depression. I wanted badly off this picture but had no earthly idea how to do it without totally disrupting my life. My first attempt to act out my personal crisis was to disappear for a day. I got in my car and drove south with no real understanding of what I was up to. In the back of my mind I could feel suicidal thoughts forming, but I kept pushing them back and driving on. I remember getting to Long Beach where nearly every motel is named after the Queen Mary, since it's been docked there for years as a commercial attraction. I guess I wasn't that far gone yet since I really was thinking I am not going to suffer the indignity of being found dead in some tacky motel called The Queen's Retreat, so I continued until I got to Costa Mesa, a nowhere mall of a place in Orange County where I did check into an anonymous motel, got something to eat and sat around the room trying to figure out my dilemma. There's no question that years of drugs and alcohol abuse had contributed greatly to this confusion about how to survive another day. A clearer-headed, more confident me would have just asked for the day off and not run away from home. I do blame Norman and Patrick a little, however, to the extent that their natures were to infantilize those of us who worked for them. I was always meant to feel that they were doing me an enormous favor by letting me be their slave because I was so lucky to be working with the best. Needless to say, most of this dynamic was infested by Patrick, but I always felt it came from the top and in a truly ironic way Patrick suffered the same abuse from Norman.

I decided I had to call the office to let them know something about my whereabouts, as it was so bizarre for me to have just disappeared. I guess I underestimated Norman's concern because he himself got on the phone immediately and tried to jolly me out of my obvious blues. He made a classic Norman remark after finding out where I was. He half joked that "I would have expected you to go, Charlie, you know, someplace beautiful like the San Ysidro Ranch" (an exclusive resort outside Santa Barbara). I knew that was his way of trying to lighten things up and talk me down so that I would come back safe and sound. We hung up and I decided to go ahead and stay overnight and go back the next day.

There was strangely no discussion of my inexplicable behavior upon my return, which only served to make me more paranoid and uncomfortable. Mary was the only person who couldn't hide her obvious feelings that I was really losing it, and I sensed that she started pulling away from me more and more. Looking back I can't blame her in the least. I was blaming most of my misery on the work we were involved in, and of course there was so much more to it than that. However, I had three weeks of seeing coiled ropes around the studio and thinking about hanging myself, coming home to a bathroom and kitchen of sharp objects and thinking of slashing my wrists and, of course, always considering overdosing on some drug which, at the time, at least would have had its compensation. And then one morning, on my way to work, I decided that I just couldn't face another moment of advice and drove my car into a brick wall

166

near the studio at fifty miles an hour. I had, however slipped on my seatbelt at the last moment and managed to total the car but not injure myself beyond some bruised ribs. I was taken to the hospital and then sent home for a few days. I'm sure during those days, pretty much everyone figured out that I was really fucked up and probably had a hard time figuring out how to deal with it. Somehow, after three days' rest, I returned and got back into the swing of things. The crisis had passed and I was determined to make up for my insane episodes.

The movie was pretty hellish to make in frozen northern locations in the middle of winter. At some point Fred and Patrick stopped speaking to each other, and we were working in an armed camp. I carried most of the messages between them, and often suffered the consequences of being in the middle. Tim Hutton tried his best to be believable in the role against ridiculous odds, and John Lone turned out to be genuinely brilliant. It was his picture and Fred knew it.

Toward the end of shooting we moved to Vancouver, British Columbia, to do the studio work in an abandoned bridge building factory. There was no sound stage large enough for the set that Fred wanted for the scientific enclosure that housed the Iceman called the vivarium. The unlikeliness of this facility existing in the Arctic tundra was so great that we later had to loop in a number of explanatory lines to try and make sense of its mere existence.

It was at this same time that Norman saw a play in New York called *A Soldier's Play* written by Charles Fuller. He loved it and got Warner Bros. to option the rights for him to direct a movie version. I was going to be the Associate Producer of that film as well. Somehow, I knew that was going to be a much more rewarding experience, and I also knew that Patrick was going to be so involved in finishing the post production of *Iceman* that I might really get a chance to get my teeth into a project. So for a while I left Vancouver and segued to working with Charles Fuller on the adaption of his play for the screen and started to have the most satisfying experience in my career to date. Once Patrick sensed that I had abandoned him, even at Norman's orders, however, he was on the warpath and jealous as hell that I was working on a picture with Norman and for the moment he wasn't going to be there to make mine and everyone else's life miserable.

Many months later when *Iceman* was completed and opened, Fred was back in Australia. I knew the Friday night it opened, from a box office service to which we subscribed that it was an absolute bomb. Many critics liked it, but then Fred had long since been the darling of the film critic community and once

168

again garnered near rave revues for a film that the public virtually boycotted. I came into the office Monday morning very depressed about the opening weekend business only to be greeted by our irrepressibly cheerful receptionist with the news that Fred had called from Australia and that she had given him the weekend figures. I didn't know what figures she was talking about until I went inside my office and on my desk was a mockup of a trade ad for a potential Tuesday morning announcement that *Iceman* had made thirteen million dollars on its opening weekend and that there was no end in sight for this cash gusher. Candy was so pleased she had been able to help. I took god knows how many tranquilizers and made the unavoidable call to Fred to give him the straight scoop. That was no fun. I remember thinking then and there that unless I can work on a picture of which I can be really proud or one that at least made tons of money there's little point in being in the industry. Fortunately, *A Soldier's Story*, as the film came to be titled, fell into the first category at least. It gave me hope, as well as one of the sexiest days of my life. Not bad considering a mere three months earlier I had plowed directly into that wall figuring life held no more surprises for me, certainly not good ones anyway. It just goes to show, you never know. Well, almost never anyway.

MY ONE AND ONLY

A Soldier's Story needed a leading man of the glamorous old school Hollywood movie star variety. Howard Rollins, Jr. had burst onto the scene with his performance in *Ragtime,* for which he was nominated for an Oscar. Norman and I agreed that he was our most likely candidate to play the key role of the college-educated black military lawyer who comes to a Southern army base to investigate the murder of a tyrannical sergeant. The other key roles in the film were also to be played by black actors, as the story was about a company of black soldiers preparing to go into battle in World War II. In most cases, those roles could have been cast three times over, judging from the extraordinary amount of talented black actors we auditioned in L.A., Chicago,

171

and New York. But this part reminded Norman of the Sidney Poitier role in "In the Heat of the Night" and he knew he needed a superstar.

I flew to New York to meet with Howard Rollins, Jr., informally, just to get a sense of him as a person before we made an official offer. Of course as the meeting, which was to be lunch at Mr. Chow, was arranged through his agent, there was no mystery why the Associate Producer of the most significant black picture of its day was flying across the country. I walked into the restaurant and Howard Rollins, Jr. was there at the table. I recognized him and introduced myself as I joined him at the table. We proceeded to have a tremendously relaxed and enjoyable encounter, talking about his work, my work, and any number of other topics that made us laugh and feel surprisingly comfortable under the circumstances. This was, after all, something of an audition for him (and he knew it) and probably the most important professional task I'd been sent on (and I knew it). But we were both pulling it off as if it were just another lunch at Mr. Chow. Aside from his obvious charm and social skills, one could hardly not take note of the fact that he rated up there with the most beautiful men alive. It was a time in his life when he was gleaming. Everything was going his way and it showed. I thought I did very well not to just sit there and stare at him. Quite the opposite, I played my role very well and when the lunch came to a conclusion, I expected to say goodbye, return to L.A. the next day, and report to Norman that we had our man. As I paid the bill, he asked me where I was headed as one often does in New York so that the possibility of sharing a cab can be determined. It turned out amazingly that we were both going to meetings in the same west side building. He was going to see his accountant, and I was meeting with Liz McCanna and Nell Nugent, two theatrical producers who held the movie rights to an Anne Tyler novel called *Dinner at the Homesick Restaurant.* We'd had innumerable telephone conversations about the possibility of Norman directing the film that they were hoping to produce based on the novel, which just happened to be one of my favorites. Howard and I laughed about the coincidence of all this since he, of course, knew Liz and Nell very well, and shared a cab across town with the idea that he would meet me in their office after his meetings since mine would probably go on longer than his. Actually my meeting was pretty brief because Liz and Nell were intent on how this rambling novel could be successfully turned into a screenplay. They were less interested in a director than a screenwriter, and I had not really come prepared to deal with that extensively. Howard did manage to join us at the end, which they enjoyed, and then he and I left together.

173

I had tickets to *My One and Only,* the Tommy Tune and Twiggy musical that night and hadn't yet asked anyone to go with me. Before we parted I conjured up the courage to ask Howard if he would like to see it, and he accepted without hesitation, saying that he had several friends in the cast and had been wanting to go. We were to meet at the theater just before curtain, which by now was probably only three hours hence. So we finally parted ways after what was meant to be a professional lunch meeting. Something else seemed to be happening.

At about two minutes to eight I was standing alone on the sidewalk in front of the theater figuring I'd been blown off. I was disappointed but not terribly surprised. After all, I was dealing with an actor, not a breed known for its dependability. Just as I'm about to enter the theater somewhat crestfallen, Howard rounded the corner on the run, dressed in a beautiful beige suit over a matching open silk shirt. It was a vision that I will be unlikely to forget. He was full of apologies about his tardiness and we rushed in, just in time for the overture. At the intermission he asked if I was hungry, which I was, and suggested we skip the second act and go to dinner at a beautiful little Italian restaurant around the corner. He did say that we had to make it back in time to go backstage as if we'd seen the whole musical and see his friends in the cast. I was certainly game. Dinner was Delicious

174

but more than that, it was fantastically flirtatious on both sides. I imagined we'd had a little to drink by the time I was confident enough to say something I don't remember saying to anyone, certainly not to an actor I was probably going to be working with in a highly professional position. I asked him if he was straight. His response was so cryptic, that to this day I never really understood it. He said, "Well, Charlie, let me put it this way. I'm about as straight as the Santa Monica freeway." Now I had lived in L.A. for years and drove that freeway daily back and forth to work and knew only too well that it's straight for miles and then makes some very definite curves here and there. I didn't press him, as the energy between us was telling me something much more direct than this riddle of an answer to a question I was somewhat embarrassed to have asked. I decided to just go with the flow, never my best skill.

We rushed back to the theater in time to go backstage and congratulate everyone on their performances, half of which we'd been there for. Honey Coles, a fabulous old black tap dancer got us totally stoned on the biggest joint I'd ever seen and then we went to George Sanford Brown's dressing room. He was the third lead in the show and an outrageous character. Something of a mad queen type, he took one look at the two of us and said they were all required to stay in the theater for two hours of photo calls that night for advertising shots and that he sensed the two of us desperately needed to spend some immediate time alone together so he was going to lock us in his dressing room. Before doing so, he pulled back a curtain in the corner and indicated a bed that we should make full use of. He was an angel and we were in heaven. The room of course was full of mirrors and we were young and beautiful and completely stoned and proceeded to make insanely passionate love. The funny thing is that for the next two hours this experience was accompanied by a constant loudspeaker calling for "Twiggy, Twiggy and Tommy for the splashing scene" or "Twiggy for the crescent moon shot please, report to the stage please." It made us giggle at how silly it all was. Amazingly, I never gave much thought, also, to how unprofessional.

I returned to L.A. the next day and confirmed Norman's hopes that Howard Rollins Jr. was the next Sidney Poitier. Needless to say, that's all I confirmed, although as the making of the movie ensued I got the distinct feeling that Norman suspected that something more than a purely professional contact had been made between Howard and me. He never confronted me on the issue, and I willingly receded into my job as Associate Producer and discontinued any other involvement with the star of the movie. I was no fool and on top of it, the star had reversed the well-known "casting couch" on me and had used his clear, sexual prowess to secure the most sought-after movie role for a black actor in decades. Whatever the case may be, it was one goddamn fantastic day that I don't regret for a minute, even though I was walking such a precarious tightrope at an important point in my career. But the honest truth is in my sixteen years in the business it was the one and only time I engaged in anything of that sort, and it was a blast. No wonder so many dreamers end up in Hollywood. It's a place where dreams really can come true, about one in a million.

177

LOWER COMPANIONS

I reported back to Vancouver for the last two weeks of shooting on *Iceman*. Upon my arrival I went into Patrick's office to say hello and fill him in on the casting progress on *A Soldier's Story*. I had barely opened my mouth when he told me to "get the fuck out of his office." I was nearly paralyzed with shock. As I retreated to my office I tried my best to figure out what could possibly engender such a greeting from my boss. Sure he was threatened that I was slightly less under his thumb than I'd been for the previous seven years, but that was just a natural maturation process on my part. It was his own goddamned fault

179

for promoting me if all he wanted was a drooling supplicant at his side night and day to carry out his often irrational orders.

Certainly I'd never been so upset in a business situation and because I'm not made of stone I really fell apart. Here I thought I was running around, doing such a good job (with the exception of one lapse of good judgement), but I'm convinced that it was not my imagination that only because I was gay the traditional producer/star tryst was taboo. At that very moment the female lead in the picture, Lindsay Crouse, wandered into my office to welcome me back warmly. We had become very friendly over the making of the film, and she had heard on the set that I was back and came right over. I burst into tears, which I suspect is not what an actor is looking for in an authority figure on a particularly difficult film, she heard me out, although there was little to say as Patrick's attitude, always unpredictable, was not inexplicable. She did the best she could to console me and left no doubt worried as to just how we were going to limp to the finish line, because, of course, this was not the only crisis on the picture. Making a film is all about crises, but this one just happened to be mine and felt more personal than professional.

I had met a guy in L.A. before I left for Vancouver who I had really fallen for, and it seemed to be mutual. We had met at a friend's house over lunch and ended up together in the

180

proverbial hot tub, but it wasn't until later that night at a party in Malibu that Chris made his interest in me clear. He was so handsome that it didn't occur to me to make a move on him. He suggested we take a walk on the beach in the moonlight. He was supplied with a good store of cocaine and got me very high before he suddenly kissed me. I was high and happy and with an amazingly sexy man who made it clear he was very interested in me. That was all a lot of fun.

Chris was a Set Decorator and we had mutual friends in the industry. We started an open affair that was enormous fun if overly drug crazed, which was making it pretty hard for me to keep my professional act together. I somehow managed (or so I thought) and when I left for Vancouver there was no question that he was going to join me there as soon as he could. He had some work to finish, and I had what I thought was a job to do on a big picture that was about to wrap.

When the shit from Patrick hit the fan I receded into my hotel room and total drug abuse and didn't even show up for work most of the time. I had a few allies on the picture, all of whom were worried to death about me, but they were busy and there wasn't much anyone could do to help. The only thing on my mind was to get Chris to Vancouver so that we could be together no matter what was coming down with my work. By

181

now I think the drugs and the situation were pushing me into a full-blown manic episode. For Chris's visit I moved into a penthouse suite with a sweeping view of Vancouver Harbor and for some unknown reason stocked the refrigerator with among other things pomegranate juice, not something I would ordinarily buy. I guess it just looked festive.

We were so happy to see each other when he arrived. I told him more of the ongoing saga on the way in from the airport and then took him up to the glamorous suite I'd arranged for our visit. I had intentionally left the curtains closed so that I could sweep them open and blow his mind with the view. Well it worked because he nearly flew from the window back to the kitchen area shaking with fear. He suffered severely from a fear of heights, not a fact one normally gets to in the first few weeks of a mad love affair. I felt so badly for him and embarrassed that I had overdone things as is often my way. To calm him down I opened the refrigerator door and offered him a glass of pomegranate juice. He turned white and almost fainted. Leave it to me to have fallen for a total stud who was not only fantastically vertiginous, but also claimed to be lethally allergic to pomegranates. Good work, Chuck. We managed to find ourselves into the completely unthreatening bedroom, and the rest of the visit was bliss. However, word got out that I had a guy staying with me from L.A. and this apparently fueled the fire that was raging inside Patrick. I only found out later that he called Norman to tell him that I had someone with me (Jesus! They'd known I was gay for years), and he wanted Norman to deal with it. I was starting to understand what big babies I'd been working for all those years and knew that sooner or later I wasn't going to be able to take it anymore. So the movie wrapped, Chris and I flew back to L.A. together, and he went to work on a Goldie Hawn picture called *Swing Shift*.

There was a long weekend coming up and I planned a romantic getaway for Chris and me at a beautiful little hotel in Santa Barbara. The plan was that I would pick him up in Malibu where they were shooting and we would leave from there. When I arrived there was something really tense going on that I had no idea had anything to do with me. I saw Chris for a minute, who told me he was too busy to even talk to me for at least an hour. As I knew both the director and the star of the movie I hung around visiting with them while Chris finished his tasks. Then in the parking lot he came to me and announced he wasn't going with me and, in fact, didn't want to see me anymore. This statement was as abrupt and inexplicable and hurtful as Patrick's had been weeks earlier. Of course it felt like it wounded me much deeper at the time because of the particular nature of our relationship when in fact my more significant problem was really with Patrick.

I tore off in my overpowered Mustang convertible up the California coastline in tears of rage and sadness. I just couldn't believe what was happening to me and didn't have a clue what I was going to do about it. Of all people, when I checked into the cozy little bungalow I'd arranged for us, I called Howard Rollins in New York. He was very sweet and spent hours with me on the phone talking me down. He convinced me that it was Chris's problem, and that I was obviously better off without him. He was right, of course, but I now had to figure out some way to repair my working relationship with Patrick because my diversion had been taken away from me, and I was forced to face the serious career crisis I was in the midst of.

When I got back to L.A., where Fred was cutting the film with a wonderful editor named Billy Weber, I slowly but surely worked my way back into Patrick's confidence. I also decided to follow my friend Gregg into AA because I knew that my drug and alcohol abuse had gotten totally out of hand. Looking back there's a very good chance that I had no idea how much of a problem that I had been creating for others, most importantly Patrick. God knows, it was no explanation for being so suddenly dropped by Chris, as his habit made mine look like child's play.

184

So for the next few years I made nearly daily trips to rooms full of sober alcoholics sharing their experience, strength and hope and being of service to others. I only wish there had been some kind of program for Patrick (Completely Out of Your Mind Anonymous perhaps). As for Chris, he was out of help's range. I came to be taught by "the program" that he was what they called a lower companion, someone in your former life with whom you shared your addiction. You were practically ordered to remove any such person from your "new" life. Chris had taken care of that part himself. But god, what I would have given to be back in that penthouse with my favorite lower companion, high as a kite, thinking we were going to feel like that forever.

WAKE-UP CALLER

Once I had been clean and sober for a few months my mind was clearer about a number of things. I knew that I was going to have to make a move from working for Norman and Patrick eventually, and that I should also start looking for a new living arrangement. I had been living with Bridget in that funny old house at the end of the dirt road for years, very much cut off from the world. Life there with Bridget had protected me from so much that I had cherished its isolation. My relationship with her had been something of a parallel to the isolation of the place itself. She and I lived up on top of the hill, looking down on the world and holding ourselves above most of it. It was high time I jump in and risk a bit more, get more involved in life and stop

187

hiding from it, as comfortable as that often was. I loved Bridget, but she and I both understood things change. I'm not sure Gregg had the same understanding, since he seemed the most affected by our triumvirate breaking up.

The market for buying a house in L.A. couldn't have been better, and I seemed to have job security again, at least as long as I wanted it anyway. I contacted a broker and told him I was looking for a house in Silverlake, the community just west of where I'd been living. I chose Silverlake because I particularly wanted a house designed by one of the three or four architects who had done most of their work in that area in the thirties, forties and fifties. Having studied architecture in college I had some knowledge of modernism and in particular what was called California Modernism of which Richard Neutra was the known master. I told the broker that I was looking particularly for a little Neutra house and gave him an idea of what I thought I could afford. He was openly skeptical about the likeliness of finding anything by Neutra that I could afford, but said he would be happy to keep an eye out for me.

I didn't hear from him for three months and then he called and said the owner of a very small Neutra in Silverlake had just dropped her price by thirty thousand and it was now closer to my stated price range. I drove over to see it during my lunch break and committed to buying it that day. There was no question but that it was going to be my house. It felt as if it had been built for me, an almost uncanny sense of predestination. I went to the broker's office and worked out the financial realities of making a serious offer and then went back to the office. I asked to speak to Patrick about something personal. He heard me out as I explained that I had found a modest but very special house to buy at a great price and was asking the company to loan me ten thousand dollars so that I could put together a down payment by adding that to what I had and what I needed to make this work. Patrick was not immediately enthusiastic about helping. I think I probably pressed and eventually got my way. I then went to my father for the same amount. He reasonably enough wanted to see the house before he committed to this extraordinary structure, pausing, and saying in his uniquely imperious manner, "Well, I can see what you would like about it." That was a positive statement from my father, believe it or not. I knew he was going to help me, and that I was now going to make this work. I was tremendously excited.

The owner of the house turned out to be a woman in her mid-twenties from a very rich Pasadena family who had joined a cult in Northern Oregon. She was apparently a "seeker" and was selling the house which she had bought with her twenty-first birthday inheritance because she wanted to free herself of all her worldly goods and live a purely spiritual life. That was great for me because she threw in all of the furniture, the washer and dryer and even some of the art, which was in rather good taste. It was a very brief negotiation period in which she came down ten thousand dollars on the asking price. Our concluding conversation was on a conference call including both of our brokers and the seller, born Carol Brook Jeffries, but now known as Ma Anad Sanamdra, her cult name. Remember, I was, after all, buying a house in Southern California.

The move really did alter the relationship with Gregg and Bridget in a noticeable way. Much more with Gregg because he not only didn't have his little Sunday night family dinners to depend on, but I think he was either envious or threatened or both by my definitive move toward adulthood. He was still living a life that wasn't that different from when he was the editor of *The Crimson* at Harvard. On top of it he was going through some pretty dramatic changes by getting sober and starting to realize that he and I had been engaged in a highly codependent relationship for years. Bridget, on the other hand, seemed to take the change very much in stride, as she did most everything, and on her visit to the house made a quick tour and announced it was perfect for me, "Just like a little white rat's maze in a laboratory."

190

This of course was a comment on how differently we liked to live, she on the relaxed and messy side, me obsessively neat and clean. There are plenty of mutual friends who still can't believe we managed to cohabitate peacefully for so many years.

During the escrow period I used to drive by the house almost every evening to admire it on my way home. One night there was a young woman in a pink jumpsuit moving some small items out of the house into her jeep parked in front. Since I knew a little about the cult I guessed it was the owner as all the women in the cult were required to wear pink. I introduced myself and she couldn't have been nicer. She gave me a very detailed tour of the house (which in fact I had only seen once that first day) and filled me in on any of its history of which she was aware. She also told me after our hour together that she was happy we had met because she thought of the house as a very spiritual place and had the feeling she was passing it on to the right person. I didn't know about that, but I enjoyed her and the chance to find out more about what was going to be my first real home of my own.

A year of living in the house went by, during which time I never tired of its beauty and serenity and significant architectural quality. I was home one day when the doorbell rang and standing, completely unexpected on my doorstep was Carol, aka Ma Anad. I asked her in and as we sat down to visit I asked her

191

where she had been during the previous year; I knew from my broker that she had left the cult just before escrow closed which had been a great relief to me as I wasn't wild about supporting the purchase of more Rolls Royces and machine guns for her guru. I had heard she was going to India to find further spiritual guidance, but until this unexpected visit, I had no real news of her. Her response to my question was, "That is of no importance," said in a strange monotone, followed by "We have these things to tell you." Oh boy, I knew I was in for something now. I kind of prepared myself for anything and asked her to please continue. She explained in the same eerie voice that she had gotten no further than Hawaii on her journey where she discovered that she was not human but was an extra-terrestrial. She went on to explain that there are two kinds of E.T.s on earth, Wake-ups and Walk-ins. It turns out she was the former, a Wake-up, meaning that she had always been an extra-terrestrial, innocently birthed by an earthling but only became aware of her "reality" (or woke up) at the appropriate time in her spiritual development. Walk-ins reportedly would enter a human body once again when the spirit inside that person had prepared itself for the change. She went on to tell me that her name was now Astredia and that she reported to Avatar who was "on the craft."

192

I sat listening politely, fully aware that I either had an insane person in my living room or an extra-terrestrial. There didn't seem to be any other choices. Things, believe it or not, got stranger. She told me that what she had come to do was to "recognize" me. Apparently, this was a technical term in her lingo that meant that you too are an E.T. (of either sort, I suppose). She had me almost sweating bullets by now wondering how I was going to get this being out of my house when she announced with great seriousness that "Once you have been recognized the process has begun." She explained that Avatar was going to be in touch with me directly because he had something special to tell me. She intimated that it was about AIDS and that on their planet they understood why this plague was sweeping across earth in a devastating way. I was starting to really lose patience now because she was touching on a subject that I really didn't wish to discuss with someone from outer space. Fortunately this visitation drew to an abrupt end when she asked for the two main pieces of art she had left in the house and disappeared as unceremoniously as she had arrived. I couldn't help but wonder how the art was going to look on the craft. And I never heard from Avatar, thank god.

193

THE BIG SCARE

A Soldier's Story was nearing completion when I was suddenly admitted to Cedar Sinai Hospital with a raging fever of 106 degrees. I had been in Santa Barbara for the weekend with Gregg and by the time I got home I was suffering from such severe chest pains that I couldn't get up from my bed without assistance. Gregg was completely freaked and rushed me to the hospital. Since this was 1985 and I was gay there was an immediate assumption on the part of the medical staff that I had pneumocystis pneumonia, the viral pneumonia that was one of the two diseases at the time that indicated fully blown AIDS. I

195

hadn't been tested for antibodies to the virus yet and therefore didn't know if I was HIV positive.

Actually, at that time, progressive doctors were recommending against being tested since there was no therapy for the disease and one just ran the risk of losing a job or an insurance policy or the support of one's family or any number of other negative scenarios. There was no plus side to knowing one's status, so an informed doctor would recommend to any patient who was in a high risk group to simply behave as if he were positive and be responsible in any sexual encounter.

I was so sick for the first few days that I played no personal role in this drama except to lie there as one doctor or intern or resident after another examined me and discussed the situation gravely with my father and step-mother off in the corner of the room, not realizing that I could often make some sense of their conversations. There was no question that I was in a life-threatening situation. My father and step-mother, Nina, used some of her influence at U.C.L.A. to find me the top man available in infectious disease, which by then was a euphemism for AIDS doctor. His name was Dr. Ralph Hansen and he was a terrific guy. I had been under the care of a Beverly Hills doctor known for his willingness to prescribe controlled substances at the drop of a hat. I had, of course, not seen him since I had gone to

196

AA, but he was still my doctor of record. So it took some doing and a few torturous days to get rid of him and get Dr. Hansen on my case, who immediately ordered a bronchoscopy in order to determine the nature of my pneumonia. This is a very unpleasant procedure where a miniature camera at the end of a long tube is lowered into your lung, as well as some device to biopsy a piece of the lung so that an exact diagnosis can be made. It was living hell except that I was such a drug addict that even with my throat stuffed with equipment, I was trying to indicate to the anesthesiologist that I needed more Demerol and liquid valium in my I.V. I'm sure he'd faced this before and stuck to his guns and I got through it, just wasn't as high as I'd like to have been.

It took several days for the results of this procedure to be verified. I was feeling a bit better and so I was fully conscious that I was awaiting a possible death sentence. So was everyone around me and at most times it was a highly charged, emotional roomful of people, some able to pretend more bravery than others. I stress roomful because an amazing number of loving friends came to my side, all of them having to suffer the indignity of wearing masks and gowns in my room because we were still in the dark ages of AIDS and the panic around the possible infectious nature of the disease was still full tilt. Many of the nurses wouldn't even touch me, and I generally felt like a leper.

The news was good. I had a severe aspiration pneumonia that was not AIDS related and would be very likely to respond to a full house of intravenous antibiotics. I remember I was often still pretty out of it and had a wonderful black nurse some of the time who would come in to the room to change the I.V. bag and refer to the medicine as "Aretha My Sin." It was only later that I understood that the antibiotic was erythromycin. She was a rare bright light in the otherwise impersonal and phobic bunch of nurses who cared for me. This was long before there was such a thing as a special AIDS ward staffed by sympathetic and informed care givers, so I was on a floor with other patients suffering from upper respiratory ailments, including lung cancer. I was, however, still kept in isolation even after the results of the bronchoscopy cleared me of having AIDS. I think in those days, if you were gay and had pneumonia, nobody but your doctor was likely to be sophisticated enough to understand the situation.

I was in the hospital for seventeen days and had collected quite a roomful of paraphernalia: flowers galore (studio expense accounts), a music system, a video tape player. It became quite the party room, and I was starting to exhaust myself with all the entertaining. I actually needed to go home finally just to get some rest. The day I was being discharged, I remember my doctor coming into the room and picking up a few of the audio tapes near my bed. He told me that he was also a fan of the Australian band INXS. I remarked how hip it was of him to know that it was pronounced "In excess" and asked if he had teenage children or something. He looked down at me and smiled ironically and said "Charlie, I'm younger than you are." Boy was that ever a turning point for me. To have had my life saved by a highly trained professional specialist who was my junior. What's next? A lawyer, dentist and accountant younger than me. You got it. So I had to spend the next few months getting the word out (as Mark Twain apparently said) that "The reports of my death have been greatly exaggerated." I would show up at social events and often see reflected in the eyes of acquaintances, "Gee, I thought he was dead." I rarely bothered to explain to anyone of no real import to me that it was just a big scare, but it was the beginning of a very depressing period for a lot of us where every cough and sniffle was being analyzed and discussed by people who knew very little on the subject. It was also the beginning of a period when serious and fatal diseases were wiping out our friends and loved ones in frightening numbers, and we who were involved had to go into high gear just to stay up with the available information as to why or how this incredible thing could be happening.

199

Although I've never been a separatist of any sort I did start then to unconsciously separate myself from people who had no understanding of or connection to AIDS. As far as I was concerned they were living on another planet, and I was now in a parallel world that was full of people fighting for their lives and suffering the loss of such young friends and loves. My personal nightmare began with a false alarm, but there was nothing false about that alarm waking me up. Nothing was ever going to be the same again.

LUNCH AT HOWARD'S

Several months later I was in New York showing the finished print of *A Soldier's Story* (1984) to the press. I was there for a week of screenings so that we would be sure that all the important media had the chance to see it. At some point, I had made contact with Luis, who was at that time a literary agent at ICM in New York. We made plans to have lunch on what was going to be my last day in the city. There was one more screening that night, but it was kind of a catch-all event and not one I felt I needed to be there for, so I had booked myself back on an afternoon plane to L.A.

When the day came I spoke to Luis in the morning, and he asked me if I would prefer to have lunch at The Russian Tea Room or at his friend Howard's office. Having never had lunch at the "glamorous" Tea Room, I took this to be a typical Luis-style joke and said, "The Russian Tea Room, of course." He slyly indicated that we should go to his friend's office instead as if, as always, there were some secret to life that only he knew. I was slightly puzzled but agreed, and we made the rendezvous arrangement. I hung up a bit disappointed as I pictured pulling a chair up to some guy named Howard's desk to share a tuna sandwich when I could be hobnobbing with the greats and near greats at an infamous industry watering hole.

Howard's office was in the Time Life building, and I had agreed to meet Luis at one o'clock at the bottom of an escalator in the lobby. When I arrived I saw a sign that indicated that the escalator was going to carry us privately to the Gilman Paper Company. On the way up Luis dropped the info that his friend Howard was Howard Gilman and he owned the company. I don't know why I expected less, since Luis had made a life out of knowing such people.

From the moment we entered I knew I was in a place far more glamorous than the Russian Tea Room. The design of the reception area and the part of the office I saw on the way to the private dining room was very handsome and obviously done with the assistance of a talented architect. The walls were hung with an extraordinary collection of minimal art, representing all of the great artists of that milieu. Luis was apparently such a regular diner there that his arrival was simply announced by the receptionist, and he and I went unaccompanied into the dining room. We were seated at a table dominated by a beautiful Cy Twombly canvas on the largest wall. A waiter entered and asked what we would like to drink and handed us a printed menu that offered a choice of entree. Needless to say a half of a tuna sandwich was not one of the choices.

Shortly a woman arrived who entered talking to Luis and only drew breath long enough to be introduced to me. She sat across from the two of us and left the head of the table for Howard, who she explained had been slightly detained. Her name was Natalie Moody and from her stature and demeanor I took her to be a very high placed executive in the company, which immediately impressed me, since this was early enough in the women's movement that such a thing was still rare. She immediately asked the waiter for the phone to be brought to her and inquired as to what the chef had made as a first course. It was soup and since Howard was still not there when it was served a plate was placed over his bowl in order to keep it hot.

203

Natalie discreetly interrogated me as a way of conversation while we ate our soup, still waiting for the mythical Howard. She was charming as hell and as extroverted an individual as I'd ever run across. She was an odd combination of a powerhouse of an executive and a little girl. She seemed so excited by the fact that I worked in the movies and on top of everything knew an old friend of theirs, Wallace Potts, who was also in the business. Luis in typical fashion sat like a cat who'd swallowed a bird, sensing he'd made a hit as Natalie seemed to approve of me. Obviously, I was not the first guest he'd paraded through their executive dining room.

Finally the door opened and in walked a very distinguished looking silver-haired man in his early sixties, buttoning his suit jacket and apologizing for being so late. I rose to be introduced and noticed immediately an intimacy and shyness in Howard that seemed like such a contradiction. As he shook my hand he looked me straight in the eyes, his face quite close to mine and whatever he said it was very welcoming and completely put me at ease in this otherwise totally strange world. We sat and Natalie proceeded to catch Howard up a little on what we had discussed, mostly my Hollywood background and the apparently fantastic fact that I knew Wallace. Howard was delighted at this news, as Wallace was clearly a very special friend who had lived in New

York for several years before I knew him, in a guest apartment of Howard's. Both Howard and Natalie missed him terribly and spent the rest of the lunch deciding what I could bring back to him from them.

The next two hours seemed to fly by with endless laughing and storytelling. To put it mildly, we hit it off. I had never before or since been so taken by anyone as I was by Howard, who I took to be a very important businessman with the demeanor of an innocent child. Natalie as well proved to be irresistibly appealing and had the clear knack of doing about twelve things at once, including prompting stories from me, a person she'd met only moments before Howard, primarily for his amusement. I was fascinated and fully engaged in the process at the same time. I was amazed that these two people could share such childlike qualities and still run what must have been a major business, judging from the little I'd seen of it at that point.

Toward the end of lunch, which was Delicious and prepared by a chef Howard had hired away from The Four Seasons, it occurred to me that they might like to see *A Soldier's Story* that night. They were Delighted and accepted excitedly. For some reason we had talked very little about the film at lunch, and it had only come up as I was leaving. I told them that I happened to be working on the same studio lot as Wallace at the time, so since I was going directly to my office from the airport, and he would probably be working late, I would be happy to bring him something if they had come up with an idea. I think it was Natalie who gleefully suggested that their chef, Goro, quickly make a huge batch of mashed potatoes with extra butter and cream (apparently Wallace's favorite thing in the world) which would be the ideal care package from them. Howard concurred, laughing at the thought of Goro's mashed potatoes being hand Delivered across the country directly to his dear friend. I was Delighted to be of service after such a wonderful and surprising experience.

We said our good-byes and I left the office feeling as if I'd fallen through the rabbit hole. I had no idea if I'd see these two people again but I couldn't remember a pair who'd made such a strong impression on me. I sensed it wasn't the end of the story as I stepped into the studio limo with Wallace's mashed potatoes in hand.

Wallace was overjoyed five or six hours later to receive the hand-Delivered treat and told me a little more about Howard and Natalie. He clearly adored them and missed being in New York terribly. He also told me that I lucked out on the Delivery, since once a lunch guest had apparently innocently asked if there was anything he could take back to L.A. for Wallace, and it turned out to be a set of four used tires for his car.

Howard didn't drop a stitch. No more than three days later, I received an incredibly charming letter describing in great detail how much they had loved the film and that they were fantastically impressed when they saw my big front screen credit as Associate Producer. It turns out they had much smaller expectations of what my function might have been on the film, as I had apparently never explained. I was too busy having fun to impress them with my industry status, which I never took very seriously anyway because I knew how absurd it all was. But they fell for the big billing and I think it was especially charming to them that I had not prepared them in any way. In any case it was certainly the kind of wonderful, old-fashioned correspondence that requires a response. I wrote back that I was delighted that they enjoyed the film and that I would stay in touch with them and hoped to be in New York again soon. Howard, being the only person in creation who writes thank you notes for thank you notes, wrote back to insist that I do so and so I was right, the story was not going to end at lunch at Howard's.

EPILOGUE

Pictures, Poems, and Text

209

Charlie with Goldie Hawn

Howard Rollins Jr. and Charlie on set in Culver City

Charlie at White Oak with a baby cheetah

Charlie holding the neighbor's puppy

And yet, though Charlie's written story does end with "Lunch at Howard's," this lunch in real time was the beginning of his life-long friendship with Howard Gilman and his new journey as Vice President of the second largest paper company on the East Coast.

A Soldier's Story, released in 1984, was Charlie's last big-release Hollywood film. He made two Disney Sunday movies: *Student Exchange* (1987) and *Parent Trap Hawaiian Honeymoon* (1989). As symptoms and illnesses started getting him down, he quit Hollywood and accepted the position in Howard's corporation, Gilman Paper Company, with offices located on a designated floor of the *Time Life Building* in New York City. Howard had promised Charlie excellent medical coverage for life—no matter what, and a job description that was too hard to resist.

Charlie's first assignment would be assisting Isabella Rossellini in her endeavor to gather and preserve the archives of her father, the Italian film maker, Roberto Rossellini. Charlie and Isabella would meet and travel together to Italy to work on this project. Thus, too, Isabella and Charlie became life-long friends. When she spoke at his memorial, she talked about how she resisted the relationship, knowing already the likelihood of his painful and tragic end. But, she said, she failed to resist because "Who could resist loving Charlie?"

Once again, Charlie catapulted from entry-level to vice president, running the philanthropic wing of Howard's company, giving money to heart disease research (Howard's malady) and the arts (Howard is credited with pushing photography into its place as fine art), and doing various tasks utilizing his production and design skills.

With his affluence as a VP for Howard, Charlie found a dream house, literally a small penthouse on the top floor of a pre-war on Christopher St., cattycorner to Stonewall Park. He was in heaven with a direct view of the Empire State Building and the city skyscape from a generous sized patio-balcony for which he employed a gardener, the gorgeous and caring Yani, who eventually became a devoted love interest and personal helper. It was Yani who answered the phone for Charlie in his last two years. I knew Charlie loved Yani in spite of the fact that Yani couldn't be on time, couldn't be exactly what Charlie wanted him to be. But like Charlie, who could resist Yani? What a sweet, gorgeous man.

For the first year or so of Charlie's job with Howard, Charlie was commuting from L.A. to NYC on a regular basis. He hadn't yet bought the place on Christopher St., hadn't yet given up entirely his Hollywood dreams. But then, he was done. The virus was a cold-hearted reality. Howard's offer was just too good. In New York he found good doctors and settled in to win the race against time.

Howard's company, inherited as a business from his father, one which he'd turned into a mega-corporation, owned an old pine-producing (paper) farm in northern Florida called White Oak Plantation. Charlie would go there from NY for business meetings and to further Howard's philanthropic endeavors in the arts and sciences. My siblings and parents were all invited to enjoy the wonders of White Oak. People's eyes used to glaze over if I spoke of White Oak because it just wasn't fair that some people could go but not everyone. It had been an elegant hunting estate in the 1700s. Under Howard's reign, the plantation housed not only a large thoroughbred business with horses worth millions, a dance studio for Mikhail Baryshnikov (White Oak Dance Project), organic farms with green houses to feed guests and the seventy-five workers, a building known affectionately as the Big Game Room with bowling alley and a private theater for movies, several swimming pools, boats at the dock on the little St. Mary's, lodges built in the 1700s, but also, and most notably, the second largest endangered species zoo and conservation project in North America. Charlie loved having his nieces come have the time of their life at this magical place. The zoo still is home to white rhinos, Siberian tigers whose owners had tired of them and maybe two dozen other species: giraffes, cheetahs, and okapis, to name a few. White Oak is ongoing today as a conservation center in Yulee, Florida, with tours available to the public.

My daughters were at the age to fit in and find total Delight in every moment visiting their Uncle Charlie at this place—a house with a zoo! Howard was a gracious host to us and always had me sit at his side in the dining room. Can you imagine? At times it was Isabella and her daughter Elettra, Misha (Baryshnikov), Charlie, and us. Whoever was top dog at the table would have the little brass bell for summoning the help from the kitchen.

We had maids who did our beds, laundry, and provided anything we needed. Crazy, coming from my, at that time, often impoverished state as a teacher in New Mexico public schools. When my husband went to White Oak with us, he played golf with Misha on Cedar 3. After the assignment to work with Isabella, Charlie had been asked to design a small golf course at White Oak Plantation known as Cedar 3. Misha and my husband Randy played at about the same level of advanced duffer, and the celebrity issue didn't faze my husband in the least. I, however, found myself barely able to speak around Misha. One time I was doing laps in the dark-blue tiled pool outside the big lodge where we were staying (Misha had his own permanent suite there). Misha came out and hopped in the pool, and when

218

he and I inadvertently were on opposite decks, me wrapping quickly in my towel, he stopped, struck a pose and flexed his million-dollar arm at me. My heart went fluttering and we both smiled. Sweet!

During his years of full-on-battle with the virus, Charlie was as unlikely a CEO as he had been movie maker or lumber baron—no training in either area; his career was built on charisma and humor. Charlie's salary was sufficient such that (he told me) he "gave" his Richard Neutra house to the dear friend who had been caretaking and restoring it to full glory. The Neutra house in the Silverlake neighborhood of Los Angeles, which Charlie told us about in "Wake Up Caller" appeared in *Elle Décor* in 1995, just after his new digs on Christopher Street had also been featured. Charlie's sense of vintage movie styles translated well into interior design. And Charlie had watched a lot of movies. One of my jobs as a young teenager was to turn off the TV in the den and encourage him to go to bed.

In Charlie's near-the-end years, he had Delusions of grandeur about his friend Isabella making a documentary of his life, but in reality, there were no takers for this project. This idea of being celebrated on film before his looming death by AIDS was imaginary—the mischievous work of his AIDS persona, Charlie Silver. Charlie Silver, however, frightened people. When Charlie spoke to me about this fantasy film that was going to start production any day, I took it lightly as if he were my little brother telling a fib (which he actually was), not unlike telling our neighbors when he was four years old that our father had given our mother a full-length white mink coat for Christmas. In reality she received a set of Revere Ware pots and pans that made her cry.

His name in lights in the credits on several movies would be his mark, the tangible spot that Charlie left for the audience of random film aficionados. Always ambitious for change and thrills, Charlie decided to produce his own life story in the form of writing vignettes. He asked me how to go about doing this on the phone one night, sometime in 1995, as I was writing my own memoir at the time. He had tried a class at City College and simply felt uncomfortable, his body too thin already, his story too eager to burst from him. Once he got started, he rented a small apartment outside the city with a garage for his 1966 Mustang convertible, a writer's hideaway. I told him just to write like he tells stories. Jump right in, leave out the boring, focus on the surprise, the vivid imagery, don't toss out the emotional, be honest, let it be funny when it's funny (five-minute university). Not a problem for this novice writer, already a master story teller. I am amazed at the collection he accrued in more or less eighteen months, before he was simply too exhausted. Somehow he managed to write between his bouts of AIDS-related dementia. The writing is readable and brisk and ended when he became too ill to write. Too homebound and stuck, putting his efforts into dying at home, not a hospital where no one would want to be with him.

The last time we were all at White Oak, Charlie could barely leave his room. He had a rocking chair to hang out in, but spent most of his time dozing off. That was spring break in the early 90s. For a pick-me-up, as he often did, he blew some of his savings (some thought this might be Charlie Silver at work) on an enormously posh beach house on Martha's Vineyard. He also sent plane tickets to me and my girls and my sister Gretchen. Needless to say, it was a thrilling idea. He had us booked for a week near Menemsha, in a three-story faux Victorian with a lap pool on the deck. I sensed there might be some problems, however, when he picked us up at the tiny airport in a rental car suitable for four, not five, and then proceeded to drive like a maniac down the long stretches of quiet country roads. He wouldn't slow down. He was raging with his gas pedal, and I finally screamed at him loud enough to convince him to pull over. If he wanted to kill someone, I explained it couldn't be with my kids in his convertible, nor did I want to experience his killing some child or animal in the farmland we were cruising through. I offered to walk or call a cab. He apologized later, but that was the end of his driving for that week at least, and maybe forever.

One of our very few falling outs. He finally apologized, realizing it was terrible behavior. Ninety miles an hour? On the quiet, country road in Martha's Vineyard?

The first morning of our stay, we saw in the daily paper that not only were Bill and Hillary on the island but also Kurt Russel and Goldie Hawn with their passel of kids. Charlie called Goldie, somehow—he must've guessed where they'd be staying and plans were made for lunch at Charlie's. Wayde, Charlie's nurse and helper, went up to the second-floor hall phone near my room and called his mom. I could hear the whispers.

We had a meeting about what meal to produce and who would go to the docks and get the seafood. I was to make a beet salad (big *faux pas* on my part when I actually grated the steamed beets on a free-standing chopping block from the 18th century). At one point, the paunchy, scraggly-bearded Kurt came to the kitchen side door and asked "Is this a smoking house?"

I had to say no, but I told him I thought the third-floor balcony would be ok as that was Charlie's hangout, and I knew Charlie was enjoying tobacco during his dwindling remaining days. Who wouldn't? After the lunch, Wayde really laid into me for being such a retard about the beets, but he had, he said, managed to remove the stain with bleach. Charlie and Goldie went off on a walk on the property and sat under some trees

222

alone for a couple hours just catching up. The kids, including Kate Hudson, played Monopoly.

At lunch Goldie reminded Kurt he had a movie coming up and to lay off the seconds. Our crab and mango dish, with the beet and blueberry cold salad was a hit. Afterwards we all went to a private beach that Goldie had permission to use. It was pleasant, a family kind of visit. Gretchen and I watched Goldie paint her toe nails. (This was pre-nail salon fervor). Charlie was happy to be with family and friends.

The following day we shopped in the little town at the other end of the Vineyard—Gretchen did the driving. Charlie bought me some huge thick towels with Vineyard monograms and got the kids Black Dog stuff. Most of the rest of our time there, he was on the third floor. The next time I would see him would be on Fire Island, the summer of the following year, his last summer.

The girls and I flew out to New York the summer of '97 and went directly from the airport to the ferry to take us across the bay. Charlie had apologized in advance for the shack he said he'd rented at The Pines on Fire Island, but of course, it was paradise to us. There was plenty of room, even a room for his cook, Todd, and a tiny guest room for me. The girls had no problem with the two sofas in the glassed-in living room.

The beach was sunny and warm, mostly gay men, lots of gym boy physiques and older corporate types wearing nothing but penis jewelry. I warned the girls that we were going down the boardwalk where just about anything could be going on in the bushes (as Charlie had warned me) and onto a clothing-optional, mostly gay men's beach. They didn't quite get why I was telling them that, but we all enjoyed sunning amidst the guys who didn't even see us. Invisibility! When a small family of men and a boy about my older daughter's age came ambling along at the surf's edge, the boy couldn't keep his eyes off of Lena. We both laughed. "Well, there's a least one straight guy."

When we said goodbye from that five-day visit, I felt and feared it might be our last goodbye. But I stuck to the no-sad-faces mandate. Charlie was on the protease inhibitor drug therapy, but the wasting had set in prior to the drug coming available. He was in his eleventh year with HIV, and his dream of coming out ok was appearing to be just that, a dream. We sat face to face on the grey-wood bench on the deck and looked deeply at each other. I didn't cry. It had been ten years since he'd said, "I'm the one who will suffer the disease; I want you to treat me just like you always have." And I agreed and I stuck to it. It was a good way to hold the love above the turbulence. A wise trick and a fairly simple rule for me to follow.

But we did have one more visit after The Pines on Fire Island: one where I invited myself. Our sister Gretchen had been living in a sublet apartment directly below Charlie's penthouse for about four months, one semester at Parson's to be precise. Charlie had provided financial aid to Gretchen two years prior so she could fulfill her dream of going to art school in Portland. During her second year of studying painting in Portland's best art school, PNCA she entered the competition to win a semester of a studio class with NYC artists that Parson's sponsored. Each art school could send one student. Gretchen won the honor and would be in New York painting for a semester. In a lovely way, she was able to help our brother who had helped her fulfill her dream. She would be the much-needed family member living very close through the tough time he was facing as a man far-gone with AIDS. The woman who lived directly below Charlie just happened, coincidentally, to be looking for a suitable renter for six months while she sojourned to Italy. It seemed like divine intervention putting the pieces together. Gretchen would be on call, would use the service stairs just outside her door to run up in the morning with his breakfast and in the evening bring him dinner and share her adventures in the Big Apple. Charlie's nurse Wayde would be there daily as assistant in all other management issues. Yani spent time there too, and for a while, there was Todd the cook, until according to Charlie, Gretchen

225

let him go. I decided I would bring my 12-year-old daughter and spend the ten days we had between Christmas and returning to school, giving Gretchen time to go home and manage her affairs. Parsons upon request had amazingly given her another semester of studio space so she could stay on as caretaker of our brother and yet have her own thing to do. Charlie requested that no one would be in his face, sitting around waiting for him die.

By the time Ursula and I arrived Dec 26, 1997, Charlie wasn't leaving the house. He was in fair humor, full of love and mischief. The first morning as we sat at his table in his apartment, he said, "So, I suppose you don't have any money, right?"

"Um, yeah, right," I agreed. He asked Wayde to come close, and he whisper-requested that Wayde go to the ATM and get $500 in small bills. I wasn't paying much attention, but when Wayde returned, giving me quite the judgmental stare, Charlie counted out two piles, equal in every way, and turned to me and Ursula saying, "This is for you and this is for you, and what I want you to do for the next ten days is to go out every day and have fun, then come back and tell me about it." Again, pretty cool instructions. I had no embarrassment about my finances. Charlie was the sibling who'd gone for the gold, and he disliked hippies in every way. He had been the one who cheered me on through a late-in-life education, having kids, and ambitions as a writer. I was Delighted at Charlie's plan. He always had a good plan, and he loved being uncle to my kids. When we got out into the hall, Ursula, who'd never seen so much cash, asked if she could save hers and we could just spend mine. I was ok with that. And hilariously, when we got home that night to tell him about our day of walking through the park and going ice skating, he asked me how much of the money we'd decided to save. We laughed. Charlie and I and the girls always laughed. Our funny bone was one big family bone we were happy to share.

On New Year's Eve that year, 1997, the three of us watched the ball fall from inside his little penthouse television—the lights of the city twinkled through every window. His hand shook as he poured our sparkling apple juice into fine champagne glasses. It seemed that it might be a last New Year for him, but we were feeling glad to be together. Ursula so wanted to go to Times Square, but we were Charlie's support team that evening—the rest had bolted as soon as they knew we'd be covering for them. Ursula demurred, knowing it was a very special night to be with Uncle Charlie.

When the call came, in March, weeks after Ursula and I had returned home to work and school, it was Gretchen telling me the details. He died at home, relatively painlessly having saved any use of pain meds for the big day. He rested on his grey velvet sofa with his helpers and friends and sister surrounding him, and then in the dusky twilight, he left his body and went to the next stop, where he sincerely hoped to be given a lemon-yellow Porsche to ride the heavenly waves. I think of him often, heading out into an ocean sunset in this ultimate vehicle, perhaps with our dad who'd earned navigation papers before his passing. Our guys, our angels. Rest in peace.

At Charlie's memorial, for which my sister and I were picked up in a limousine from Charlie's building, the eulogizers had been informed that one of Charlie's last wishes was that everyone who spoke would say something humorous. And Charlie got that wish.

The manuscript arrived a while later in my mail at home. After reading the first few pages, I decided to put it in the bottom of my big desk drawer. Twenty-one years later, it was time to bring it out and honor his story, framing it in my words, adding Bridget's poem, and two of mine, Gretchen's sketch, and a brief retelling, from what I knew, of his life after "Lunch at Howard's."

Merimée

Funnily Enough
by Merimée

Yes, *funnily*; I finally looked it up
thinking to have one up on you
but funnily, it is an adverb, one which forever
makes me think of you, funny, like when you

talked about flying from Spain to Fire Island for a party
and the Senegalese water taxi dude
had you walk across waist-high water,
suitcase and shoes held high
your tie perhaps just skimming the city block to shore
the dark water flickering beach house reflections

Funnily, the party was the next night anyway—

The hurricane howled against sheet-glass windows
As you regaled us that night
but we didn't move, fixed, I'd say, to your story

Funnily enough, you wrote later that our visits kept you going
Friends did stop dropping by
Christmas alone with the fever at 105° waiting for a dinner
promised by Howard; you said he did show up, finally—
A couple of years of this

you in New York, us in New Mexico
too far apart, but the wires worked well, funnily

And that last summer at The Pines,
we sat on the gray weathered deck, close;
it was time to go
You were luminescent, your eyes so open,
so fatless on your Bowie-like face
so surprisingly round like tiny dessert plates

hand-blown glass, blue, and of course, Italian

You were beautiful, funnily enough,
so thin and pale under your tan
with no need to speak of death;
you really didn't care for un-fun plans

Now, anyone says "funnily"
and I see that freckled face, leaning forward, half-smiling,
your white terrycloth robe, your eyes reflecting the bay,
that happy thatch of dirty blonde hair
so California, still so Hollywood, still you—
in striped-blue pajamas, or pale blue vapors or
walking on water, funnily enough,
if you really wanted to.

A POEM FOR CHARLIE
by Bridget Byrne—sent to Charlie's memorial.

A Modernist urn, I learn.
Perhaps the perfect space to hold
your bold soul.
But, without doubt, you will spill out
flooding into our memories, informing our present,
inspiring our futures,
never far from our minds because of all kinds of things you loved:

The daylight fading on Cedar 3 as the final putt dropped;
Enthusiasms which could not be stopped;
Animals' soft ears and quizzical eyes;
People with much better thighs;
Cashmere sweaters, perfectly folded;
Opinions which could not be molded
by convention or propriety,
but were enlivened by hilarity
and an off-kilter kind of charity;
Yellow birthday cakes;
Witty double takes;
Late night dates and impossible mates;
Mom's macaroni and cheese;
Blanche's head upon your knees;
Candles burnt at both ends
which shed a glorious light;
The view from Penthouse F, day or night;
Sun and sea water;
Stimulants you didn't oughta;
White tulips with unfloppy stems;
Elegant writing pens;
Movies and music, companions and cars;
The latest thing in bars,
gyms, fashion and folly;
No-one who was falsely jolly;

Picture frames properly aligned;
Taste imaginatively refined;
Gilman World, with Natalie and Howard;
And things that should never have been said out loud . . .

The struggle for perfection
is no easy talent to possess,
but for us who loved you best
and miss you now, you've found eternal rest,
I hope you always understood
that nothing in the world is so good in the end
as a perfect friend.

And, dear Charlie, it's a fact. You were that.

Love always, Bridget.

VELVET COUCH IN A ROOM WITH NO CURTAINS
(a pantoum) by Merimée

You sat all day then called to tell
He went to sofa, morphine sleep at last
He so skinny, wide-eyed, wasting
couldn't tell when AIDS would rest

He went to sofa, morphine sleep
Manhattan sky over paper Narcissus
AIDS, rude game, never shouted "Uncle"
small Village penthouse, his upturned palm

Manhattan lights through paper Narcissus
Empire State's red spire on black
Village penthouse an upturned palm
Did spirit fly or burst to pure bright white?

Spired Empire red against night
You called at 3 our brother gone
Did spirit fly or burst to pure bright white?
Quietly, you said. Rest, then he was gone.

You called at 3 our brother's gone
We watched him all day into night
Quietly, you said. He rested then was gone.
You, Yanni, Wayde were dark and still

with him, the blue-eyed blonde, so skinny
You, Yani, Wayde, hearts beating, still,
sitting all day you called to tell
We surrounded him until his spirit's flight.

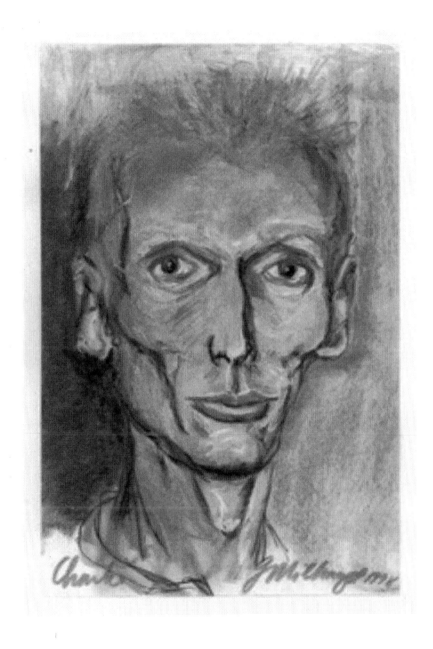

Drawing by Gretchen

GRATITUDE

Many thanks to my family and friends: Lena, Ursula & Robert, Georgia, Jennifer Simpson, and Randy, for typing the original hard copy. Thanks, Ursula, for waving your magic wand and doing final edits. And to Kirstie for finding good fixes. Also to Justin who gave electronic translation from the vintage photocopy his best shot. And to Irene for sending me the manuscript twenty-two years ago. I'm glad it wasn't lost. Special kudos to Larry Schulte who edited and advised and encouraged.

Thanks to Sony Studios for the permission to use the Howard Rollins Jr. Columbia Pictures promo photo. Thanks to Georgia Santa Maria for scanning and touching up the old photos. Thanks to Gretchen for allowing me to use the sketch of Charlie that is even more stunning in its original color. Thanks to Lauren Thompson for allowing the use of her very Hollywood font called "Champagne and Limousines."

Special thanks to Charlie for being such an angel brother to me and my kids and the rest of the family. It is so wonderful to have been loved by a brother who made me feel special all the time, every time.

ABOUT THE EDITOR

Merimée is Charlie's older sister by three and a half years. She was writing a memoir and poems when Charlie was ill and gave him a few tips when he evinced an interest in writing his own book. She did not, however, get to see him sing with the Hammond Typewriter. Her comment disparaging his singing happened in a different setting. She says they never had any other squabbles other than that unfortunate comment.

Reading a *Mad Magazine* together as the family traveled home to Oregon from Disneyland was where she learned that her little brother had a great sense of humor and was very skilled at making her laugh. Before that, he hadn't existed in her radar. She was fourteen and he eleven. From that point on Charlie was one of her favorite people. She found him to be supportive, not judgmental, and they spent a great deal of time together in their adult lives. He was a godfather to her kids. The only copy of his stories came to her at his wake, when a friend was quoting from it at the memorial. The manuscript then sat untouched in a drawer for 21 years.

www.MerimeeMoffitt.com

Made in the USA
Columbia, SC
05 February 2020